Enterprise System Platforms

Platforms

Transforming the Agenda

JOHAN MAGNUSSON

ANDREAS NILSSON

 Studentlitteratur

Art. No 38299
ISBN 978-91-44-09670-4
First edition
1:1

© Studentlitteratur 2014
www.studentlitteratur.se
Studentlitteratur AB, Lund

Fact checking: Gustaf Juell-Skielse, Anders G. Nilsson
Cover design: Adam Dahlstedt

Printed by Graficas Cems S.L., Spain 2014

CONTENTS

PREFACE

During the past decade, we (the authors) have time and time again found ourselves in situations where we felt that the very foundation of understanding with regard to the intersection of business and information technology (IT) needs to be addressed. During this time, IT has undergone a number of radical shifts: from exclusive to inclusive, from product to service, from uniform to pluralistic et cetera. Corporate IT has to a large extent failed to respond to these challenges, with the result of sub-optimized use and diffusion.

The echoes of these failures can be seen in examples of project failures, loss of revenues and steadily increasing spending on IT. The press is always fast in highlighting these failures, resulting in a situation where risk mitigation and aversion becomes the principal code of conduct. In other words: despite technology constantly moving forward, institutional forces manage to counteract the reaping of benefits associated with organizational use.

This book is our humble contribution to a solution for this Gordian knot of technology in the corporate context. We approach this ambition from the perspective of the very core of corporate IT, i.e. enterprise systems. These systems (such as Enterprise Resource Planning and Customer Relationship Management) constitute the infrastructure for organizational value creation, encompassing the lion's share of processes and transactions within and between the corporation(s). In combining findings from our research into enterprise systems and platform strategies, we show how the market is currently evolving, how IT could be used to avoid tradeoffs between economies of scale and scope, and how a turn to platforms brings with it both great expectations and a clear new set of drawbacks.

The intended target group for this book consists of both students and practitioners of enterprise systems. For students, this book adds both introductory knowledge and insights into the world of enterprise systems, as well as into the shift to platforms that the market is currently experiencing. This includes both students of technology and business. For practitioners, this book adds applied knowledge related to how vendors, consultants and users should navigate their respective businesses in relation to the current shift in market.

About the Authors

Johan Magnusson holds a PhD in Accounting, a Licentiate degree in Informatics and a Bachelor's degree in Psychology. His research concerns the delimiting and regulative aspects of technology, and he has published extensively on the issue since joining the academy in 2002. His current research involves platform strategies, IT governance, enterprise systems and interactive visualization of big data. He works as director of the Centre for Business Solutions at the School of Business, Economics and Law, University of Gothenburg, and as associate professor at Westerdal Oslo School of Art, Communication and Technology. He is also active in the industrial community both as board member and advisor.

Andreas Nilsson holds a PhD in Computer and Systems Sciences and works as a researcher at Stockholm University. His main interest lies in industrial transformation towards platform-mediated collaborations, both in the public and the private sector. Andreas has combined academic and industrial work since 2001 and has been actively involved in several startups of companies and research initiatives as advisor, researcher and manager.

Acknowledgements

Johan Magnusson: I would like to thank Andreas for the recurring patience in assembling white jigsaw puzzles, as well as the Torsten Söderberg Foundation for the monetary support necessary in writing this book. In addition to this, I would like thank my wife Maria, and our two sons Theodor and Amos for (for want of a better word) accepting that I am, at times, far, far away.

Andreas Nilsson: I would like to thank Johan for his unmatched passion and capability to produce high-quality text under very stressful circumstances. Also, I would like to thank Frida, Isabelle and Samuel for not throwing Dad's computer out the window.

In addition to this, we would like to thank the many colleagues that have been part in writing this book. These include individuals from both academia and industry, and, in particular Prof. Anders G. Nilsson and Asoc. Prof. Gustaf Juell-Skielse for their thorough work in reviewing the book.

Arkösund, Sweden, September 2014

Johan Magnusson & Andreas Nilsson

Today every organization has an enterprise system. What started in the 1970's as standard packages for large industrial firms has now spread to firms of any size and in any business sector. Who would dream about starting a business today without proper IT systems for managing customers, suppliers and employees and not to forget accountancy? And who has the time and money to develop these IT systems on their own instead of going standard?

Standard packages represent a shift in how software is developed, distributed and implemented. They are ready to install and designed to meet requirements of several users and using organizations. They provide economy of scale and embody experience and knowledge from earlier implementations. Large software vendors are also better positioned to keep pace with technological development than user organizations.

But to implement and use an enterprise system is a complex process that has proven to be both lengthy and costly. Up to 80 percent of all implementations fail. That's why service orientation is so compelling. Today you can assemble enterprise systems from software services delivered by different suppliers. And you can start instantly without years of installations and rollouts and you only pay for what you use. But again, enterprise system as service is standard. And although configurable, standard software hampers the flexibility of the individual firm. What you gain in implementation speed and reduced development costs you lose in flexibility.

In this challenging book Johan Magnusson and Andreas Nilsson open the curtain for the new wave of enterprise system platforms. Enterprise system platforms catch the long tail of individual business needs while leveraging the shared needs of many users. It changes the conditions for everyone involved:

user, owner, and innovator. The authors show through dyads of value creation how the actors' agendas are transformed.

The authors are well versed and knowledgeable in both enterprise systems and platforms and cover important characteristics, definitions, theories and approaches in the field. The book is largely based on up-to-date research and on the authors' academic activities in mainly Gothenburg and Stockholm. They also provide clear and well-founded classifications and taxonomies that provide an educational structure for the material presented in the book.

The book is a valuable contribution to the field of IT and management and is well suited for academic students as well as for practitioners. It is easily read and logically structured with illustrative figures and tables, interesting educational exhibits throughout the book and valuable historical briefings in the field. The areas of enterprise systems and platforms are in a fruitful manner linked to the established disciplines of management information systems and business. The book can therefore be used to advantage in training within information systems, iSchools and in various economic disciplines.

Stockholm University, September, 2014

Gustaf Juell-Skielse, associate professor, and Anders G. Nilsson, professor

PART 1

Foundations

CHAPTER 1

Setting the Scene

In this chapter, we introduce six underlying forces that have impacted the design and use of IT in recent years. The purpose of this is to set the scene for the reader, and provide a background to the concepts of enterprise systems and platforms that are the focuses of this book.

The Six Forces of IT

In Figure 1.1, we summarize the underlying forces that are descriptive for these past few years' evolution. As seen in the figure, we have not addressed

Figure 1.1 The Six Forces of IT.

the intricate interplay and influence between the identified forces, but instead focused on describing them in a sequential manner. Albeit an interesting aspect of the development, we have refrained from this level of analysis for the sake of readability and to avoid the logical fallacy *post hoc ergo propter hoc*.

THE DIGITALIZATION OF EVERYTHING

This new technology, let's call it Information Technology.

LEAVITT AND WHISLER, 1958, P. 41.

Since the 1950s, the type of technology referred to as *information technology* (IT) has been introduced into more and more aspects of social life. Stemming from machinery intended for calculating large amounts of data (large in the relative use of the term) for the military, government and business, the technology was early on identified as having fundamental implications for various strands of life.

In relation to business, one of the prominent thinkers in relation to IT at the time, Harvard Professor of Accounting John Dearden (1922–1989) offered his vision of what the end-state of the current level of technological development was.

… the more information available, the better the decision. This end is to be accomplished by having vast amounts of data stored in a computer memory, by having this information constantly updated by point-of-action recorders, by having direct interrogation of the data stored in the computer's memory available to the executive, and by having immediate visual display of the answer.

DEARDEN, J., 1964, P. 128.

Readers of today may find it hard to understand the extent to which this line of thinking was radical, but needless to say we see substantial evidence of Dearden's foresight in today's business environment. The rise of business intelligence (BI) solutions and the developments surrounding Big Data seem almost eerily hyphenated in the quote. In addition to this, Dearden also highlights one of the underlying drives behind this strive for total and real-time information, i.e. rational decision making. If every physical action and event is recorded, we will be in a position where all of our decisions, in theory, will be informed and hence freed from irrational guess works. When action becomes digitalized information, we can handle it in a rational manner.

As noted by March and Olsen's dominating garbage can model and Simon's notion of *bounded rationality*, the very concept of rationality warrants further attention. Human decision-making is, perhaps by definition and default, more a-rational or quasi-rational than rational? It is not the intent of this book to take a stance in relation to this question. Interestingly though, we would advise the reader to carefully take stock of the *intent* of the information technology currently available. We believe that herein lies a proverbial conflict between the design and use of information technology. But this is something that we will have occasion to burrow deeper into further on in this book, once again returning to the works of John Dearden. This is of particular interest when we consider recent developments such as the rise of solutions for "Prescriptive analytics", with the systems themselves actually making the decisions.

Digitalization does not, however, stop at the updating of information in a "computer's memory" as noted by Dearden. It has vaster consequences, and according to some, it also brings with it the blurring of boundaries between the physical and the non-physical, between work as we have known it for years and work as we (perhaps) will know it in the future. Researchers such as Andrew McAffee and Eric Brynjolfsson (2008) note that the main attribute of information technology is the digitalization of the very atom of business itself. This atom is the process; or in other words the workflow that in aggregated form constitutes business.

With the rise of enterprise systems such as Enterprise Resource Planning (ERP) systems during the 1990s, processes are hard-coded into the very fabric of information technology *en masse*. They are manifested through blueprints, and the only way to execute a process is through the information technology interface. The upside to this is the rapid deployment of process related innovations, such as e.g. an optimal way to handle returns for a global consumer goods firm. Through information technology, this could, once again in theory, be implemented overnight leading to a homogenization and optimization of the entire firm's global process for return handling.

Through the works of researchers such as Clayton Christensen, we have started to understand the disruptive implications of IT for social and corporate life. Through phenomena such as the Internet of Things (or the Internet of Everything), more and more of what we have seen as separated from IT is rapidly becoming entangled in technology. Industries where IT traditionally has been seen as an administrative or production technology are undergoing shifts where either the entire product or service is digitalized (such as in the music industry), or IT is becoming a substantial part of the product (such as in the automobile industry) or service (such as in the management consulting industry). This shift brings with it new entrants and competitors that previously were not there, echoing the premonition put forth by Michael Porter in the 1980s.

THE STANDARDIZATION OF THE UNIQUE

Before we address the issue of standardization, we need to clarify what we are actually referring to when we refer to standardization. Perhaps the best way to do this is to clarify what standardization *is not,* to eliminate some of the common misconceptions related to this term. Standardization *does not* mean that all things are the same. In this manner, the existence of standardized processes within a firm *does not* mean that all processes are homogenous. It *does not* mean that all configurations are equal, or that variants of processes cannot be found. We refer to standardization along the lines of the Capability Maturity Model (CMM), where processes are standardized if they are described following a previously agreed upon notation and nomenclature. Hence, following technology standards does not mean that we may only use the predefined applications of technology, but that we must stick to certain rules and regulations in our application of technology. Related back to CMM, the final level of maturity in terms of standard compliance simply means that we use the same language in describing our objects (Leonardi, 2011).

IT has traditionally been geared towards economies of scale, where the organization agrees upon the "best" way of configuring a process and then selects or develops an information system to support this in an economically rational manner. This has given rise to organizations striving for what they often refer to as *global processes*, or global process templates, ensuring that the organization as a whole follows the same process for e.g. financial reporting. The underlying rationale behind this is through following a global template we ensure both economies of scale and internal communication, agreeing to one set of definitions and a common workflow. This has given rise to the birth of Shared Service Centers, or centralized "factories" handling the entire organization's administrative needs related to specific processes. The core of this idea is that there should not be any individualized customizations to the process, but that everybody needs to agree on what is set in the global template.

This poses an interesting question with regard to the tradeoff between economies of scale versus economies of scope. In economies of scale, the striving for efficiency is highlighted, whereas in economies of scope the striving for effectiveness and adaptability is emphasized. Global processes could be regarded as a concrete example of how organizations strive for economies of scale, at the potential cost of economies of scope. This brings forth the issue of agility, and the increased demands on firms not to consider competitive advantage as something than can be sustainable over time. This is in sharp contrast with previous conceptions of strategic management, in which "sustainable competitive advantage", where the resources were not easily imitated, was seen as the optimal state for an organization. Today, we are more and more turning our attention to issues such as dynamic capabilities, agility and continuous change, with "sustainable" competitive advantage being a contradiction in terms.

Enterprise systems come with a predefined set of processes, geared for creating global processes, similar to what Upton and Staats (2008) refer to as the building of a cathedral. The key to the cathedral is the issue of knowing exactly what you want, and the inability to use the structure before it is completed. Once completed, it will stand for hundreds of years, supporting the identified requirements of the past. The tradeoff between efficiency and effectiveness (or scale and scope) is clear: how can organizations with a constant need for reconfiguring their processes and business models achieve both efficiency and effectiveness through standardized processes?

THE COMMODITIZATION OF PROCESSES

One of the general trends is the shift of things traded towards commodities. In this process of commoditization, products or services that were previously customized are repackaged into commodities.

Being packaged as commodities brings with it the promise of reducing the cost involved in making a transaction on the market in question (often referred to as the *transaction cost*) through decreasing the time that a customer has to spend in selecting what she is intent on buying. At the same time, it reduces the cost involved in switching between vendors (often referred to as the *switching cost*). Since the commodity is packaged in a similar fashion by different vendors, the buyer can, at least theoretically, exit her relationship with a current vendor and engage with a new one, this without the characteristics of the commodity changing noticeably.

While the commoditization of products has been going on for quite some time, the commoditization of services has only recently been addressed on a larger scale. In 2005, Professor Thomas Davenport published a paper in the Harvard Business Review on how *processes* were currently undergoing commoditization. As Davenport argued, the rise of process standards such as COBIT, SCOR and ISO14001 bring with them a common nomenclature and language to describe the processes. This can be regarded as a first step in the commoditization of processes.

When firms can describe their processes in a manner that can be understood by actors on the outsourcing market, processes will become a commodity traded like any other one on an open market. If we as a firm, for instance, were to describe our supply chain process following the SCOR methodology, we could more easily communicate our process specifications, the expected level of performance and the cost to external parties. If the said process were to be sourced to a lesser price from an actor on the open market than from internal resources, then we could choose to outsource this particular process to the vendor most meeting our requirements in terms of price and quality.

This phenomenon of sourcing processes (or sub-processes) from external vendors is referred to as Business Process Outsourcing (BPO) and has throughout the past couple of years seen a radical increase in market size. At the same time as this development can be understood from an economic point of view, it raises several questions as to the very nature of the firm. What actually constitutes the firm as we understand it? What constitutes the boundaries of the firm? These questions touch upon the questions raised within interorganizational collaboration, as we will see later in this book.

The impacts of the commoditization of processes have also been highlighted for firms working outside of traditional industry. Christensen, Wang and van Bever (2013) advocate an upcoming commoditization of the services offered by management consultants, where we see firms such as McKinsey and Associates packaging elements of their previous delivery for faster and more efficient delivery. The potential of technologies such as crowdsourcing of analysis (e.g. Kaggle), prescriptive analytics (e.g. Ayata) and self-service BI (e.g. Tableau Software) shifts a large portion of what was previously supplied by the management consultants as a complete package. In other words, new technology-induced solutions are disrupting the very firms that have recommended firms to invest in the said technology.

THE CONSUMERIZATION OF TECHNOLOGY

Any user having been exposed to corporate IT while at the same time using consumer IT will testify to the sharp contrasts between the two. Consumer IT has experienced a drastic growth during the past couple of decades, creating a chasm within a technology that initially was designed for the corporate realm. IT was initially so complex and costly that any consumer-directed application of it would be commercially impossible. It was a technology designed for professionals, be they accountants, physicians or officers.

During the 1980s, a new wave of technology started to proliferate the market. The IT industry was starting to re-frame itself towards end users, through innovations such as desktop computing and the spinoffs this technology brought with it. In the following decade, the Internet was introduced as a medium through which communications could be made even less costly and available for a larger part of the community. In the early years, vendors strived to create value in what initially best could be referred to as an empty room. Connecting people (which coincidentally was the byline of Nokia, one of the dominant cellphone vendors at the time) and achieving network externalities, along the lines of what is commonly referred to as Metcalfe's law: the utility of a network increases exponentially with every added node.

As the incumbent vendors saw the massive potential of a market for consumer IT, they were at the same time distraught about how to feed the rapid onslaught of innovations back into the market for corporate IT. Having established themselves on a market where they currently had a strong position, they were adamant towards making radical changes to their existing solutions. Hence, the direct effects of a massive increase in innovation for consumer IT did not spill over to the corporate side.

At the same time, new challenging vendors of corporate IT saw massive potential in the new technology being introduced for consumers. In it they saw the necessary prerequisites for transforming the graphical user interface (GUI) and the way we as users consume technology. With the introduction of software as a service (SaaS) as a delivery model for software, challenging vendors often offer the intended customers the option of trying their solution out for free.

This challenges the previously so dominant position of the incumbent vendors, and opens up for a blending of consumer and corporate IT through the introduction of a new line of products and services. At the same time it creates a market for vendors that sell their solutions directly to the end user, not necessarily attending to often centralized models of IT procurement for the customer. This in turn creates a situation where a larger and larger part of an organization's total IT spending is becoming decentralized, with a lack of corporate cost control as a direct consequence. This phenomenon is referred to as "Shadow IT", and according to prominent industry analysts,

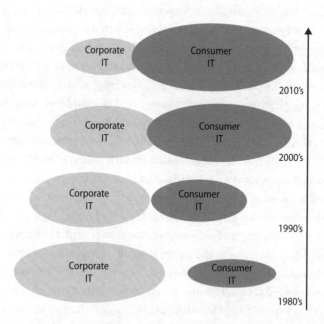

Figure 1.2 Illustration of how consumer and corporate IT have changed over the past few decades.

the proportion of IT spending that falls within the category of Shadow IT will reach as much as 90 percent by 2018. We will address this in more detail in the section on investing in enterprise systems.

THE COCREATION OF VALUE

In the shift towards cloud-based delivery models such as SaaS, we have a hard time seeing the value of our infrastructure in the books. Instead of procuring a resource, we subscribe to it, and hence we have no depreciation and no book value of the service in question. A service (such as SaaS) is in this respect something that generates value momentarily on usage, and not something that we can place in our inventory if we wish to use it later on instead of now. In addition to this, the value of a service is created in the meeting of the client and provider/service, and hence not simply created but rather *cocreated*.

In research, there has long been a strong tradition of looking into strategic alliances and other interorganizational collaborations. Despite this, there seems to be a lack of understanding in terms of which mechanisms exist between organizations involved in cocreation. This is noted by Sarker et al. (2012), in their study of how an ecosystem of partners surrounding a large ERP vendor is involved in the cocreation of value.

Perhaps the best example of the allure of cocreation can be found in Google's business model. When we ask our students (in a highly unscientific manner) about who Google's customers actually are, the answer is predominantly the students themselves, in giving them the right answers to their searches and supplying them with the service of finding value on the Internet. In response to this answer, we then ask if perhaps they might be mistaking "customer" for "factory worker", with the following logic: the students generate revenue by supporting advertising by Google. At the same time, they share their personal sentiments and information while optimizing the algorithms behind the searches. Hence, they are involved in both direct revenue generation and the accruement of structural capital for Google. As noted by Charles Baudelaire in his famous poem Spleen in Paris: "The greatest trick the devil ever pulled was convincing the world he didn't exist." Cocreation brings with it the possibility of displacing the traditional roles of producer and consumer, creating what is often referred to as "prosumers", i.e. actors involved with the parallel production and consumption of a product or service.

An alternative to this is the growth of what is commonly referred to as the *sharing* or *collaborative* economy. According to The Economist, this grew to a $26 billion market during 2013. Examples such as Airbnb, a service that supports sub-letting private lodgings to travellers, or Uber, a ride-sharing service, thrive on platform logic in connecting private owners of lodging and transportation with consumers wanting to share resources. These firms are competing with traditional channels such as hotels and taxis, as well as toppling the previous composition of services offered by e.g. travel agencies through cocreation.

THE DISINTEGRATION OF SYSTEMS

Turning and turning in the widening gyre
The falcon cannot hear the falconer;

Things fall apart; the centre cannot hold;
Mere anarchy is loosed upon the world.

W.B. YEATS, *THE SECOND COMING*

In the early 1950s, novelist and Nobel laureate Chinua Achebe described the social transformation taking place in a small, Nigerian rural village. With the inflow of new norms and influences, the social fabric of everyday life started to change, resulting in both wonderful new possibilities and the loss of that which once was.

The situation described in the novel is one of disintegration. Defined as the "shift from larger to smaller pieces", disintegration is also central to understanding what has been happening for the past 30-odd years within the IT industry, particularly in relation to enterprise systems.

Software development has undergone several shifts since its birth in the 1950s (some would argue that the development of software goes back even further, to Thomas von Neumann or even Karl Leibnitz). Central to the change in development methodology and software architecture has been the striving for re-use and loose coupling of code snippets. These snippets were first referred to as functions, later on objects and currently services. The services of today stem from a new approach to building systems first introduced in the late 1990s and referred to as Service Oriented Architecture (SOA).

SOA stipulates that a system should have the ability to use and issue services from and to (from the system itself) external systems. Hence, a system designed following a SOA approach should both be able to share its own code and calculations with other systems, and not be self-sufficient in terms of code. Hence, the exchange of services between systems (often referred to as *web services*) becomes a signifying mark for SOA based systems. We will address the technical aspects of SOA in a later chapter in this book.

In stipulating and agreeing on the standards for the exchange of the said services and the possibility of utilizing internet protocols instead of proprietary network solutions as the medium for exchanging services, the cost of integration has radically decreased on a per unit basis. The implications of SOA on IT in general and enterprise systems in particular have been an increased disintegration, somewhat paradoxically due to the increase of inter-system integrations. Since systems no longer need to be self-sufficient in terms of code and functionality, the previously so strong *raison d'être* for monolith solutions has become obsolete. With integration being standardized, it is now possible to combine services from a number of systems into one single set of functionality, without a disproportionate increase in cost.

Hence, the disintegration of systems is expressed in the increase of cross-dependencies between systems and the possibility of satisfying functional requirements through combining existing services from a multitude of systems. The consequences of this can be seen in such diverse phenomena as SaaS and Shadow IT, and a mean decrease in project scope for software development. Much in line with what Chinua Achebe described in "Things fall apart", disintegration brings with it both substantial possibilities, but also significant problems for users and vendors alike. We will have the opportunity of returning to some of these later on in this book.

Recommended Reading

In terms of further reading, we recommend the following material:

Achebe, C. (1958). *Things fall apart*. London: United Press.
Christensen, C. M., Baumann, H., Ruggles, R., & Sadtler, T. M. (2006). Disruptive innovation for social change. *Harvard Business Review*, 84(12), 94.

Christensen, C. M., Wang, D., & van Bever, D. (2013). Consulting on the Cusp of Disruption. *Harvard Business Review.91*(10), 106–114.

Cohen, M.D., March, J. G., & Olsen, J. P. (1972). A Garbage can model Organizational Choice. *Administrative Science Quarterly, 17(1)* 1–25.

Davenport, T. H. (2005). The coming commoditization of processes. *Harvard Business Review, 83*(6), 100–108.

Dearden, J. (1964). Can management information be automated? *Harvard Business Review, 42*(2), 128–135.

Jensen, M. C., & Meckling, W. H. (1976). Theory of the firm: Managerial behavior, agency costs and ownership structure. *Journal of Financial Economics, 3*(4), 305–360.

Leavitt, H. J. & Whisler, T. L. (1958). Management in the 1980's. *Harvard Business Review, 36*(6), 41–48.

Leonardi, P. M. (2011). When flexible routines meet flexible technologies: Affordance, constraint, and the imbrication of human and material agencies. *MIS Quarterly, 35*(1), 147–167.

McAfee, A., & Brynjolfsson, E. (2008). Investing in the IT that makes a competitive difference. *Harvard Business Review, 86*(7/8), 98.

Porter, M. E., & Millar, V. E. (1985). How information gives you competitive advantage. *Harvard Business Review,* (July–August), 1–15.

Sarker, S., Sarker, S., Sahaym, A., & Bjørn-Andersen, N. (2012). Exploring value cocreation in relationships between an ERP vendor and its partners: a revelatory case study. *MIS Quarterly, 36*(1), 317–338.

Simon, H. A. (1979). Rational decision making in business organizations. *The American Economic Review, 69*(4), 493–513.

Tiwana, A., & Konsynski, B. (2010). Complementarities between organizational IT architecture and governance structure, *Information Systems Research, 21*(2), 288–304.

Upton, D. M., & Staats, B. R. (2008). Radically simple IT. *Harvard Business Review, 86*(3), 118.

Woodard, C. J., Ramasubbu, N., Tschang, F. T., & Sambamurthy, V. (2013). Design capital and design moves: the logic of digital business strategy. *MIS Quarterly, 37*(2), 537–564.

Zittrain, J. L. (2006). The generative internet. *Harvard Law Review,* 119, 1974–2040.

Questions to discuss

- How will the six forces influence future corporate use of IT?
- How do the forces influence one another?
- Are there any new emerging forces on the horizon?

CHAPTER 2

Enter the Actors

Enterprise Systems

In this section, we present our definition of enterprise systems along with an excursion into how these systems have developed since the 1970s. In addition to this, we show how economies of scale have gradually been forced to give way to economies of scope, exposing a potential tradeoff between the two.

DEFINITION

Enterprise systems are defined as enterprise wide, standardized information systems. We will devote some attention to explaining the basic building blocks of this definition, and also include some critical reflections on the role of a definition. For increased readability, we will start by defining *information systems*, followed by *enterprise wide* and finally *standardized*.

Information systems

Information systems (IS) are defined as a combination of data, processes and people. Coined by Professor Börje Langefors in the 1960s, the term has been used in a variety of forms since its introduction. In the Nordic countries, IS has been used to differentiate the socio-technical from the technical, i.e. IS from IT, where there has been a strong pull towards not wanting to focus too much on the technology.

In later years, this distinction has come to be less and less relevant, since a technology such as IT never truly exists in a vacuum. Hence, IT is embedded in the social fabric of our society, transcending even the division of the corporate and private. In this manner, we could regard the technical artifact as a *boundary object* (see further description under Exhibit), or in

Exhibit: IT as a boundary object

Coined by Susan Leigh Star and James R. Griesemer in their 1989 study of the Berkeley Museum of Vertebrate Zoology in the US, a boundary object is described as something that is "… plastic enough to adapt to local needs and constraints of the several parties employing them, yet robust enough to maintain a common identity across sites …" (p. 393). Hence, it could be regarded as a link between different social worlds, allowing for a translation between the said worlds.

The concept has had a significant impact on the study of IS, and has become one of the core concepts within what is referred to as Science and Technology Studies (STS). One illustrative example of this type of research can be found in Pawlowski and Robey's (2004) study of knowledge brokering among IT professionals. Here, the IT systems themselves are regarded as boundary objects in that they cross organizational lines of demarcation. Using the IT systems hence offers a means by which knowledge transfer between different roles and departments becomes possible.

Another example of how boundary objects have been used in the study of information systems is found in Barrett and Oborn (2010), where the object of inquiry is cross-cultural software development teams. Here, the software specifications and project management tools utilized by the teams are regarded as boundary objects.

other words something that connects two different social realms. Instead, IS has been used for describing the field of research focused on the use and design of information systems and information technology, as well as the internal function of IT within an organization (Weill and Ross, 2004).

In this book we will use the term "system" to refer to a collection of software-based functionality. This is naturally dependent upon the underlying technologies, some of which are IT artifacts, as well as the context of use for the said functionality.

Enterprise wide

The second building block of the definition of enterprise systems is that it is a total system (Dearden, 1963) in that it encompasses processes from the entire organization. In this manner, it brings with it an integration of information

Exhibit: Information and Big Data

Central to the field of IS and this very book lies the concept of "information". In this context, information is used along the lines of Claude E. Shannon's (1916–2001) Theory of Information where there is a sharp link between information and message. In this respect, information decoupled from cognitive schemas, messages or "understanding" as a context are considered as data. Information could hence be viewed as contextualized data.

Börje Langefors (1915–2009) added another layer of understanding to the interplay between data, context and information in his Infological equation (1974):

$$I = i(D, S, t)$$

where D is the data representing the intended information, S is the receiving structure or pre-knowledge of the user, t is the time available for the user interpreting the data, and I is the information function. Central to this equation is the role of the preferences and pre-knowledge of the receiver. This has previously been approached through the Hegelian concept of Weltanschauung or Leibnitz's concept of apperception.

Contrasting information from data offers a potential avenue for criticism towards more recent phenomena such as Big Data and Data Scientists. Earlier developments such as that of Shannon and Langefors made the case for focusing on the value of data more than the underpinning data itself.

Some of the most profound criticism of the concept of Big Data lies in the decontextualization of use and value from data. Through Big Data, data itself is seen as the solution for a wide variety of issues, and it is in the vast amounts of real time, structured and unstructured data that we will find the solution to all our problems. Developments within Data mining, pushed on by technological developments of in-memory databases such as SAP's Hana allow us, for the first time in history, to handle the vast amount of available data as a source for information.

To make sure that organizations can utilize these vast new (assumed) possibilities through data, new roles such as that of "Data Scientists" are becoming increasingly popular. Looking into the required skill-set and how we as universities educate these prospective data scientists, it is apparent that at least currently we are downplaying the contextualization necessary to turn data into information. At present, understanding of the context of data, i.e. business understanding, is largely overlooked, resulting in a potential risk that we will ask data scientists to find patterns in our data that are potentially counter-productive.

and processes from all elements of the organization (Rom and Rohde, 2007) securing the flow of information throughout the entire enterprise.

Integration refers to both internal as well as external perspectives. In terms of the internal perspective, the software integrates several of the organization's processes into one system. This system, as in the case of Customer Relationship Management (CRM) systems, offers the user fully integrated functionality for handling various aspects related to customer relationship management. This may involve functionality that links information from warehouse to sales, or from sales to R&D, with the intent of reducing lead times and increasing the quality of decisions. In line with our introductory discussion to this book, the underlying premise for this is that the better and more complete the information, the better and more informed the decisions will be.

Despite the difference in scope of the various forms of enterprise systems used in a corporate information systems environment, the software strives to add to the linking of processes and information flows existing throughout the organization. With very few organizations of today acting in a vacuum, without external stakeholders, this also calls for an external integration.

This external integration is brought about through the integration of processes that are not owned by the organizations themselves, but that still constitute an integral part of the overall value generation. With organizations having customers, the customer's procurement process is, one might argue, at least logically integrated into the sales process of the organization. In a similar fashion, procurement in the organization in question is logically integrated with the sales of their suppliers. In addition to this, there are legal requirements in relation to statutory reporting that logically integrate the organization with other external stakeholders such as tax authorities et cetera. Hence, on a logical level, the scope of integration goes beyond the organization's juridical boundaries, and hence enterprise systems need to be externally integrated as well.

All this having been said, the enterprise systems within the organization need to connect every aspect of the business. Non-integrated software creates hand-offs between systems and users that are cumbersome, potentially erroneous and perhaps above all costly and time consuming. If an organization is to function as efficiently as possible and perform at the utmost level, integration is a bare necessity.

Standardized

The third building block of the definition of enterprise systems used in this book is that of standardized. In customized software development, the intent of the developers is to create a piece of software that in an optimal manner supports the context of use. This means that the aspiration is to achieve as close an alignment as possible between the functionality of the software and the needs and requirements of the intended use.

Naturally, this perfect alignment is practically never achieved. One of the reasons for this is that while use is individual, systems are in essence collective. Hence, the implementation of a new system for managing bookings in the joint conference room will bring with it a need for the users to comply with the system if they wish to make a booking. In this seemingly naïve example, the system is designed to support the average user of the organization. In addition to this, since systems are relatively costly to design, the vendor of the said system will want to sell it to several different organizations. Hence, the system will be designed to support various forms of organizations and various sets of users.

This brings issues of inter- and intra-firm variability into play. An individual user of organization A may share the idea about how an ideal booking is to be made with one or several individual users of organization B, and display a higher degree of variance in relation to her coworkers from organization A. Without going into detail here, once we accept the idea of standardized solutions, we will have to deal with issues related to individual compliance.

Enterprise systems contain generic functionality that could be perceived as the least common denominator of the intended contexts of usage. The outset of this is a standardized set of use-cases, where the developers and designers opt for a *best practice* design. One example of this could e.g. be seen in Microsoft Excel, the most popular spreadsheet solution currently on the market. It is not obvious that the particular means by which the software supports the handling of spreadsheets and spreadsheet related work is optimal for all users, but instead of commissioning the development of new spreadsheet software perfectly aligned to a particular user, users adapt to the particular use embedded in Excel. Similar examples of sub-optimal design can be found in the QWERTY designed keyboard, which was originally designed to delimit the speed of typing due to technical limitations in the typewriters.

Exhibit: The regulatory and constraining aspects of enterprise systems

During recent years, there has been a substantial amount of research focused on the constraining factors of technologies such as enterprise systems. This includes the work of Jannis Kallinikos as well as that of Hald and Mouritsen and Hedberg and Jönsson, which we will describe in more detail below.

In his book *Governing through technology* from 2011, Kallinikos approaches the issue of technology as a generic form of regulation, i.e. as an actor in its own right with substantial impact on the social fabric.

> … technology entails an objectified system of processes and forces that shape tasks and operations both in the direct way of embodying functionality that engrave particular courses of action and in the rather unobtrusive fashion of shaping perceptions and preferences, forming skills, routines and professional roles. (p. 18).

To put this in the context of the enterprise system, the way in which the system as such specifies how e.g. the process of accounts receivable is to be handled through both process and functionality directs the users in how to handle such a rudimentary task as how to send invoices. With the system replacing previous ways in which invoices were handled, it locks the users into a particular process. In turn, this comes with a new set of preferences for the user, along with new roles and routines. One of the implications of this is that the technology itself (here being the enterprise system) acts as a homogenizer of work, standardizing the processes internally. In their 2013 study of enterprise systems as boundary objects (see previous exhibit) Hald and Mouritsen investigate the constraining function of ERP, focusing more specifically on the aspects of operations management.

Hedberg and Jönsson wrote an early piece on the necessity of designing what they referred to as "semi-confusing information systems" to counteract the path dependencies and stability that an enterprise system entails. With the system focused on repetitive tasks and decision-making, Hedberg and Jönsson argue that managers need to be exposed to triggers that give rise to experimental behavior and rearrangement, rather than simply being supplied with what they had expected from past experience. Subsequently, Hedberg and Jönsson acknowledge the regulatory and constraining aspects of enterprise systems, and offer a solution to the problem. Despite this, we see that enterprise systems in particular have proven to be adamant towards introducing this type of a design criterion.

In this manner, we see that enterprise systems come with an element of performativity and regulation. The underlying premises and assumptions made by the software developers become part of the global use and if, to return to the example of Microsoft Excel, you wish to truncate your tables you will do so in the manner prescribed by the software.

The aspect of performativity brings with it a certain set of issues for competitive advantage in terms of the scope of the system. In the late 1990s, a certain type of enterprise system referred to as *Enterprise Resource Planning* (ERP) dominated the market for enterprise systems. This type of system comes with a fixed set of processes, i.e. the design of how the organization in question should go about doing their business. In purchasing the system, the organization in question would import a new set of processes (albeit selectively adapted). With the system also being purchased by competing firms, this would in theory lead to similar process designs in the competing firms. In an influential article from 1998, Thomas Davenport refers to this as achieving "the SAP way of doing business", after the dominating vendor at the time.

With this type of a homogenization between how competing firms conduct their business, both the operative and strategic competitive advantages of firms would be negatively affected. With homogenized process designs, they would, to use a sports analogy, run equally fast. With the same vendor, they would be stuck in the same race forever, incapable of e.g. entering a new market before their competitors. This is because they would be dependent upon functionality that would be made available at the same time for their competitors.

HISTORY OF ENTERPRISE SYSTEMS

On those remote pages it is written that animals are divided into (a) those that belong to the Emperor, (b) embalmed ones, (c) those that are trained, (d) suckling pigs, (e) mermaids, (f) fabulous ones, (g) stray dogs, (h) those that are included in this classification, (i) those that tremble as if they were mad, (j) innumerable ones, (k) those drawn with a very fine camel's hair brush, (l) others, (m) those that have just broken a flower vase, (n) those that resemble flies from a distance.

BORGES, 1974, P. 103

As noted in the preface of this book, we regard technological development as a parallel, non-sequential process. Hence, the issue of division and classification as noted in the opening quote becomes highly problematic. On the one hand, we could regard the evolution of solutions according to market logic, where they are understood as manifestations of products marketed and sold by vendors on the enterprise systems market. Unfortunately, this simplification brings with it several shortcomings.

Enterprise systems have, on a grand scale, been around since the early 1970s with the introduction of Material Requirement Planning (MRP) systems. Before this, with hardware being the delimiting factor in terms of both performance and price, software was primarily customized and bundled with the technology itself. In Figure 2.1, we summarize the development of enterprise systems from the early MRP systems to the more contemporary phenomena of Cloud-based delivery models. The reader will here note a potential logical quagmire, with the mix of a set of functionality with that of architecture, but we ask you to please bear with us a while longer. The issues of architecture/delivery model and functional scope/investments are highly interconnected, as we will soon see.

As seen in Figure 2.1, the functional scope of the products marketed as enterprise systems increased up until the mid 2000s, and after that started to become more and more delimited. This is related to the issue of disintegration.

On a general level, we can see the historical development of enterprise systems as a quest for avoiding the tradeoff between economies of scale and

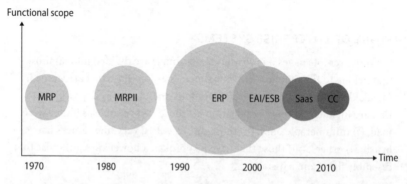

Figure 2.1 Overview of historic development in terms of functional scope of each solution.

scope. In the striving towards economies of scale, organizations have aspired for efficiency through numbers, i.e. building leaner and larger factories, increasing the size of an organization to a level where even the slightest increase in efficiency would result in massive benefits. In this endeavor, organizations have appended to a paradigm referred to as "Command and Control", i.e. striving for gaining control over all relevant resources and dominating the market thereafter.

In the striving towards economies of scope, organizations face altogether different challenges. Instead of "Command and Control", they append to what has been described as the paradigm of "Sense and Adapt", being quick, nimble and as soon as possible sensing what changes the surrounding environment is undergoing and swiftly adapting the resources thereafter. In this endeavor, organizations have aspired for agility and the ability to quickly reconfigure their business in the quest for responding to changes in demand.

As noted previously, the enterprise systems play a vital role in supporting the processes of an organization, and they have traditionally done so through standardization (internal as well as external) in a striving towards efficiency, often at the cost of agility. This constitutes an inherent paradox of IT itself, eloquently captured by Kallinikos (2011, p. 14p):

> Traditionally, the organizational use of technology has been predicated upon the model of concentration, often justified on the basis of economies of scale and calculations of costs and benefits. By way of contrast, information technologies are assumed to favor scalability, dispersion and ultimately adaptation to individual needs. The diffusion of information artifacts throughout the social fabric has therefore come to be seen as implying the decline of the logic of concentration.

We will return to this line of argument throughout the following historical exposé.

From Large to Enormous: The Bloating Years 1970–2000

Material Requirement Planning was introduced as a solution for manufacturing firms in the 1970s. The scope of this particular system was the process of requirement planning, i.e. the necessary planning, and breakdown of finished products (through the Bill of Materials, BOM) into purchase requisitions and purchase orders for the necessary material. The underlying idea was to automate as much as possible of the previously manual handling, decreasing the lead times and eliminating the element of human error.

From early on, these systems were tailor-made to fit particular organizations. Eventually, the software developers noticed that they were in essence actually building the same systems for one organization after another, and that there was a potential for standardization, i.e. packaging the systems into commodities to be more easily procured (Commercial off the Shelf, COTS).

With standardization came the notion of creating an optimized material requirement planning process, i.e. utilizing the knowledge from previous development assignments into the design of an optimal process. From this instance, the systems became associated with best practice, and we saw the birth of a new type of system: the first class of enterprise systems following the definition proposed by this book.

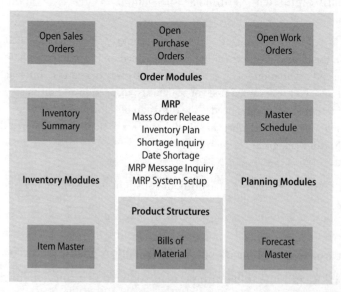

Figure 2.2 Structure and content of an MRP system.

Exhibit: The myth of best practice and its adoption

In a study of how an enterprise systems vendor actually went about creating the "best practice" functionality inherent in their solution, Wagner, Scott and Galliers (2006) showed how a small group of individuals became involved in defining what actually constituted the optimal way of doing things in the entire industry. Arguing that conceptions of best practices are transferred through templates and processes into the actual software, the authors question the ethical dimension of having a group of external experts dictate what constitutes best practice within an industry. This brings into play the political aspects of enterprise systems development, a subject that has been largely overlooked within research.

On the other side of this spectrum (i.e. the development vs implementation), Yeow and Kien Sia (2008) show that the "technological frames" of embedded best practice leads to a necessary pluralism within an adopting organization. Once again this brings into play the political dimension and negotiation of best practice as it takes place within an organization. As noted by the authors, there is a bias in research to consider organizations as monoliths in line with the implemented technology. The consequence of these findings is that best practice is always translated into the organization, much in line with the overarching theoretical claim of the Scandinavian Institutional Theory school of thought (Czarniawska & Sevon, 2005) and Rogers (2010) notion of "re-innovation".

Separating the process and application layers, the software developers quickly understood that the MRP process needed to be endowed with a certain degree of adaptability. In other words they identified variants of the process dominating certain industries, and a need for different ideal types in terms of process configuration.

This led to the introduction of a separate layer in the system, where the organization as such could choose which particular ideal type of configuration would best suit the organization. This in turn spiked the existence of what is referred to as "verticals", i.e. industry specific templates. With this, the vendors could utilize the same basic code and system to approach several different industries, having the same system cater to the needs of such diverse businesses such as for instance manufacturing and utility.

MRP systems were commercially successful, and having saturated the market during the 1970–80s the vendors were hard pressed for a new solution that could expand their market. Having invested in the basic foundation for an enterprise system, they saw the potential of expanding the functional scope of their product, catering to the need for integrated information management.

The new product that was created was in time dubbed Material Resource Management, or MRPII. MRPII involved the basic functionality of the MRP systems, along with a widening of scope to encompass additional functionality for neighboring processes in the value chain. With the vast costs associated with integrating different systems, the MRPII systems brought with them the possibility of retiring existing systems and integrations (something that was relatively expensive to set up and maintain), and also brought with it the promise of once more shortening the lead time and making the select processes more efficient through automation and rationalization. Needless to say, the business case for these solutions were hence based on the same type of logic as that of the MRP systems, and in a similar fashion they were a commercial success.

During the early 1990s the quest for process optimization through the use of information technology reached somewhat of a pinnacle. This came through the creation of what could be referred to as a total system, an all-encompassing information system that covered all processes for an organization. With the MRP and MRPII systems paving the way for an endowment of trust in the use of IT for making processes more efficient (see Exhibit, BPR), the market was seen to be ready for a new type of product, the Enterprise Resource Planning (ERP) system.

The ERP system aspired towards what no other system prior to it had done. Through focusing not on a particular process but *all* processes within an organization, it promised the complete integration of internal information and the optimal configuration of not only a selection of processes but also the complete set. In theory this would lead to an optimization of the entire organization, eliminating all sources of sub-optimization and human error through the same recipe as MRP and MRPII, automation and rationalization. With maintenance costs for the installed base at the time taking up some 80 percent of the complete IT spending, this promised not only to make the business as such more efficient, but also to aid the IT department in their

Exhibit: Business Process Reengineering

In a highly influential article in *Harvard Business Review* (1990), Michael Hammer showed how Ford managed to radically improve its accounts payable process with massive business gains as a consequence. The underlying idea was later coined as "Business Process Reengineering" (BPR), and it was promoted as a novel way of reaping the benefits of computerization, something that according to Hammer had so far not been seen.

In line with the reasoning of the article, firms are prone towards automating processes through the use of computers rather than carefully examining whether the process as such is warranted. So, instead of directly translating the processes of the firm into the enterprise system, the firm needs to be adamant in "obliterating" obsolete and sub-optimal processes, radically re-designing the processes before implementing them in the enterprise system.

Hammer was part of the "process-turn", where processes became the new atoms of the enterprise. BPR was hence seen as the link between the surge in computerization at the time, and the reconfiguration of organizations from functional to process oriented. With the scope of BPR projects and initiatives often being wide, the whole movement came to be severely criticized following ample reports of failed projects. Despite this, the adoption of enterprise systems and BPR were and continue to be highly linked, albeit BPR not currently being a legitimate acronym.

task of integrating and maintaining what was now a staggering amount of systems and applications.

With the massive functional scope, the price tag was of course far from discreet. During the period firms reported spending between 2–10 percent of their annual turnover on a new ERP system. At the same time, several firms reported massive difficulties with getting their ERP systems implemented. In some cases, this even led to the firms going bankrupt as a direct effect of the new systems not functioning properly. Examples of these massive failures can be found throughout the literature on ERP, as noted in the section of further reading and Exhibit.

With the high risk of failure, the high level of criticality and the high price associated with ERP systems, the reader might have a hard time

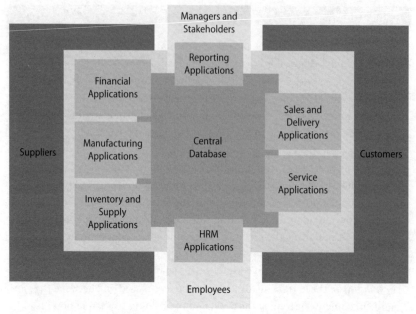

Figure 2.3 Adopted from Davenport, 1998, p.5.

understanding why firms invested in the technology at all. Apart from the issue of modernity, there are at least two reasons why firms chose to adopt ERP.

First, there is the issue of signaling. As seen in the Exhibit on the next page, firms that went public with their intent to invest in an ERP system saw a significant increase in their stock price. Hence, it was possible to justify the investment from a shareholder value perspective. Second (and perhaps related to the first), during the period when ERP systems were introduced onto the market, there was a widespread fear of what was referred to as the "millennia" or "Y2K" bug. In its most simplified form, this consisted of a fear that the systems built up to this point had failed to take into account what would happen at the turn of the millennia in terms of their internal date format. Having been built for machines with highly limited amounts of internal memory, the systems had specified the year to be comprised of two digits. Hence, after New Year's Eve 1999 ("99") there was no way of telling how the systems would react when the year would turn to "00".

There were a lot of efforts being put into redesigning legacy systems so that they would be guaranteed to function in the new millennium, yet this

Exhibit: Massive enterprise system failures

Throughout the years there have been numerous examples of failed enterprise system initiatives. One of the problems with these reports is that they are predominantly produced by the trade press, and hence have very little substance in terms of reliability. Hence, they should be taken as circumstantial rather than substantial. Nevertheless, we have decided to include a list of five of the most newsworthy global initiatives during the past couple of years, as reported by the Australian CIO Magazine.

- During 2008, the BBC launched their digitalization initiative with a budget of nearly 100 million pounds. After an audit conducted in 2012, the project was terminated and the CTO was let go.
- In 2005, the state of California initiated an ERP implementation with a focus on payroll functionality. By 2013, the project was dismantled after spending USD 371 million without getting payroll to work. The vendor and partner were sued by the state.
- In 2013, the Obama administration launched their "Healthcare.gov" initiative, inviting the public to register for public health insurance. Only 30 percent of the users were able to register due to faulty functionality, and 25 percent of the integrations with private insurance firms contained substantial errors.
- Since 1977, the Office of Personnel Management in the US have invested an excess of USD 100 million to automate and digitalize the paperwork involved in handling retirement documentation of US government employees. By 2008, the new system was in place only to be shut down shortly thereafter and the office returning to manual handling of paper documents.
- In an attempt to create the world's largest public database for national health, the UK initiated a project in 2002 with a budget of 12 billion pounds. Missing the first deadline in 2007, the project was finally terminated in 2011. According to a recent report, the project was identified as costing the British taxpayers 10 billion pounds.

was a difficult and costly enterprise involving the re-engineering of systems without sufficient documentation, built in programming languages long since forgotten by the majority of software engineers. Hence, the new breed of enterprise systems referred to as ERP, with their full functional scope

Exhibit: ERP investments and the effect on shareholder value

Throughout the years there have been numerous attempts at macro studies that capture the impacts of ERP investments on performance. These studies have primarily focused on the changes in revenue and financial performance, partly due to the fact that access has been restricted to more process oriented measures. The problem with many of these studies is that they fail to address the representational value of a firm's reported financial performance, not amply taking into account the role that financial accounting plays within and between firms.

In Magnusson et al. (2011), this is approached through a different perspective. In gathering transactional data directly from the ERP systems of five wholesalers over three years, the authors were able to link the investment in ERP with changes in lead times three years after the investment. Interestingly, the study was only to statistically establish a negative impact of ERP investments on productivity.

A separate group of studies have focused on the changes in stock price and shareholder value of firms implementing ERP. As an early example of this, Hayes, Hunton and Reck from the University of South Florida (2001) were able to identify a positive market reaction to public announcements of ERP investments. In this study of 376 public announcements, the authors could isolate several contingency factors influencing the extent of the market reaction, such as whether the ERP vendor was one of the Mega vendors and if the adopting organization was in a sound financial state.

The study raises several interesting questions, such as if the firm should aspire for shareholder value, should these findings be taken into consideration in the choice of ERP vendor? Or should we consider the time of adoption in a different light?

covering all the processes in a firm and with the promise of replacing most legacy systems in the organization, were seen as a short cut to assurance.

During the late 1990s there was a surge in investments in ERP systems. Vendors such as the three Swedish vendors IFS, Intentia and IBS saw annual growth rates surpassing 100 percent, and a vast majority of large organizations were seen getting on the bandwagon.

Following the massive investments in the late 1990s, and the often less than impressive benefits of the said investments coupled with a decrease in trust and status for IT in general, investments in ERP froze in the early years of the 21st century. By 2002, many of the major ERP vendors displayed significant difficulties in keeping up with the cost of having a large organization, and a wave of consolidation and takeover were in full effect. Vendors (such as Peoplesoft) acquired other vendors (such as JD Edwards), only to be later acquired by larger vendors (such as in this case Oracle). From having been relatively low concentrated, the industry started to become more and more concentrated, with the three vendors (referred to as "mega vendors") Oracle, Microsoft and SAP taking a lion's share of the market.

At the same time the Internet, which up to this point had been a relatively marginalized phenomenon for enterprise systems (having been more internally focused in devoted networks) started to emerge as a serious issue for corporate IT. Here, the ERP vendors saw a new chance of creating a new product to cater to the needs of their market. In a similar fashion as in the turn from MRP to MRPII, some analysts and academics started referring to this new generation of ERP systems (with increased dependence on the Internet as a means of communication) as ERPII. Vendors started to incorporate what they referred to as "e-" into their products such as "e-commerce", "e-business" and "e-government", and technologies such as WAP (Wireless Application Protocol) gave rise to new devices as a means to access the enterprise systems.

Given the widespread adoption of Internet technologies during the early 21st century, the notion of ERPII quickly became obsolete. As the Internet became a natural channel for business and a medium for communication, there was no way for enterprise systems vendors to avoid it, making it naturally incorporated into the ERP systems rather than the signifying mark of a new generation of solutions. In the next chapter we will discuss the envelopment of Internet technology into the enterprise systems in more detail.

During the same period, there was an increase in functional scope for ERP systems. The ardent reader will note that we have described ERP systems as having a full functional scope, and hence an increase in functional scope may sound counter-intuitive. The explanation for this is that the first generation of ERP systems had a full functional scope in terms of *within* the organization, not breaching the borders of the organization in terms of juridical boundaries. Hence, the first generation of ERP systems did not offer the integration of e.g. the organization's sales process to the customer's procurement process, or the organization's product lifecycle management

(PLM) process with that of the suppliers. The signifying mark of the new generation of ERP systems (stemming from the early 21st century) was that integration between the organization and its customers and suppliers was becoming more and more a necessity.

This expansion of the functional scope not only to cater to internal but also to external integration was both related to the proliferation of internet standards for communication, and organizations striving for benefits that transcended the internal processes. Instead of seeing the organization as delimited by the juridical boundaries of the firm, new metaphors such as that of "business ecosystem" become relevant as the basis for evaluating a new enterprise system.

From Enormous to Infinitesimal: The Disintegration Years (2000–)

As noted in the previous chapter, the early years of enterprise systems (1970–2000) brought with it a steady increase in the scope of functionality and complexity in the solutions themselves. From one perspective, this can be seen as a way for the vendors to increase their power over their customers. In another perspective, it can be seen as a means to support organizations in their continuing computerization and digitalization of processes.

Following the decrease in legitimacy for enterprise systems in the early 21st century (in conjunction with the IT-bust and the lack of real problems following the Y2K scare), organizations started to question the replacement of existing legacy systems with new ERP systems. Instead of exchanging the currently operational and in many cases economically sound (completely depreciated) systems with new systems that required massive resources to implement, organizations wanted to follow an alternative strategy in relation to IT. This "new" strategy was referred to as "Best of Breed", where systems would be selected on their fit, and then integrated into a complete solution. So, instead of procuring an ERP system with e.g. sub-par customer relationship management (CRM) functionality, the CRM functionality would be supplied by a solution more fitting than the overall ERP solution's. Hence, instead of having one vendor to deliver all system support, best-of-breed involves a multitude of vendors together catering to the complete needs of the organization.

This strategy requires integration being possible from both a cost efficiency and a functional perspective. Previous approaches to integrating systems was largely conducted through peer-to-peer (P2P) approaches, with the systems being firmly rather than loosely coupled. This resulted in integrations being costly, complex and resulting in lock-ins and interdependencies.

Enterprise Application Integration (EAI) was first introduced in the late 1990s in an approach where a middle-ware solution would cater to the integration and management of the said integration. In the middle-ware, the integration was standardized through Application Program Interfaces (APIs), resulting in a centralized integration with the potential for both re-use and de-coupling of existing integrations. In other words, instead of integrating all systems in a decentralized manner through customizations and P2P, EAI promoted a centralized approach for integration. The result of this possibility was a decrease in functional scope covered by each solution, and instead the organization could follow a best-of-breed strategy in provisioning their enterprise system's needs. This is considered as the first example of the previously mentioned disintegration, and effectively put a halt to bloating within enterprise systems.

In the early 21st century, the Internet was steadily becoming the new platform for business applications. New standards in the form of dialects of XML et cetera were quickly becoming accepted and implemented. One result of this was a gradual change of EAI solutions to accept the growing architectural principles of Service Oriented Architecture (SOA) and open standards. This resulted in a new stream of EAI solutions appending to a software architecture referred to as Enterprise Service Bus (ESB).

SOA infers that systems are composed of a set of self-contained units of functionality (referred to as *services*). These services can be shared and utilized between all connected systems. In line with previous design principles for object-oriented programming et cetera, one of the many benefits that this implies is that it facilitates reuse and hence a more efficient code. But in contrast to previous approaches, systems built on the design principles of SOA can share services across systems, regardless of their physical or logical location.

To illustrate this, we will use the case of a simple routine within the public sector where we show how SOA enabled systems would be able to support the routine.

As noted previously, the increased usage of web services for integration

---

Exhibit: The implications of SOA in supporting a new process

The municipality of Gothenburg offers its citizens the service of parking out in the street in the vicinity of their place of residence. This does, however, require a parking permit issued by the municipality, which in turn involves the following process:

1 Request parking form.
2 Request notice that you are registered at a certain address,
3 Request notice that you are the registered owner of a certain car.
4 Pay an invoice and receive receipt from the bank.
5 Send all documents along with the form to the municipality.
6 Wait for a decision and your parking permit to arrive by post.

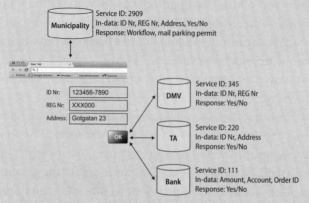

Figure 2.4 The implications of SOA in supporting a new process.

Provided that the systems of the parking authorities within the municipality, the department of motor vehicles (DMV), the tax authorities (TA) and the bank were built according to SOA principles, all requests could be automated (see Figure 2.4) and the time that it would take for the citizen to receive her parking permit would be decreased from four weeks to two days (provided the postal system works). With each system being ready to supply other systems with services, we could regard the requests as simple calls for services where the authorities could respond through a simple Boolean, yes or no. Is the person with the id number "123456-7890" registered at the address "Gotgatan 23"? Is the person with the id number "123456-7890" the registered owner of the car with the registration number "xxx000"? Is the order with the order id number "1111" paid in full? If all answers are yes, then the order is effectuated and the parking permit mailed (or rather a workflow for mailing a certain parking permit is initiated).

through SOA resulted in a radical decrease in integration costs. One example of this can be found in services such as zapier.com and cloudwork.com. These services offer you the possibility as a regular user, without any coding experience or expertise, to build integrations directly on the web. Let's say that you have a webpage with a form such as Wufu.com where prospective customers can show their interests in your products. If you are using Salesforce as a CRM system, zapier.com allows you to link the form to your Salesforce installation, automatically generating a new lead in your CRM system for your sales staff to handle accordingly. Or perhaps more arbitrarily, that you wish to receive a text message when you receive a new email in your Gmail.com account? Or you wish to automatically file for bankruptcy when you run out of cash? With the Internet straddled with a massive amount of systems that offer API integrations through SOA standards, you could basically integrate anything into anything, as long as the services have been defined beforehand within each system.

In parallel with the development and deployment of SOA, the market was undergoing a radical change, not only in relation to the increased usage of best-of-breed strategies, but also in relation to the willingness and ability of organizations to invest in IT. As a global economic crisis hit the market hard in 2008/9, software vendors had to adopt new methods of supplying their customers with their solutions. With the capital necessary for investing running more scarce, new models aspiring from the "on demand" movement, i.e. pricing and payment models, were based on a "pay-as-you-go" logic. Instead of investing in the software, making it part of your balance sheet and assets of the firm, the software is leased according to a subscription-based logic.

This particular brand of licensing is referred to as Software as a Service (SaaS), constituting a radical shift in the provisioning and packaging of software. Instead of seeing the software as a product, the software vendor has moved along the same development path as several firms within the basic industry, such as SKF, Volvo, Rolls Royce, Metso et cetera. Instead of selling a product, they sell a solution with a large portion of services appended to the initial product. In the case of software vendors, the product is the software itself, and the services relate to financing (subscribing instead of investing), maintenance and concurrent development (upgrades).

This type of packaging was not new to the software industry, and previous examples such as Application Service Provision (ASP) and Grid Computing

Exhibit: Cloud API Management

As noted previously, Application Programming Interfaces (APIs) allow for easy access between components in IT solutions. These could be considered as the gateways between various services, and hence they also form an important element of the infrastructure of any organization.

Traditionally, these APIs have been utilized primarily for internal integration projects, yet with the rise of more and more advanced service-oriented enterprise systems, they have also become an important mechanism for business development.

Organizations are realizing more and more that the amount of data related to their own line of business offers them a potential for developing additional services that would warrant revenues. Take the example of a logistics firm, which traditionally has handled the relationships with their customers through standardized reports. With their customers having their own enterprise systems, an API allowing for real-time updates from the logistic firm's system would allow for instance order handlers to service their customers more professionally.

Hence, APIs offer an avenue for business development, yet with the multitude of APIs steadily growing, the continuous management of the said APIs becomes an issue in need of attention. One solution for this need is through firms delivering "Cloud API Management" services. Firms such as Intel's Mashery.com and Apigee.com are just the some of the first movers within this field.

are two of the main predecessors. Hence, one could argue that SaaS was merely a new coat of paint on a previously existing solution, i.e. a refurbishing of the brand if you so will. We would argue against this, with SaaS being more than a distributed off-site running of the systems. Instead, it is a decomposition of what was previously referred to as a system into a bundle of services delivered to the customer (or client). At the heart of the SaaS movement within enterprise systems provisioning lies the disintegration that we have introduced previously in this book, with a radical decrease in functional scope from each and every vendor, into smaller chunks of functionality offered as commodities on the market. Subsequently, we can interpret SaaS as being either a new way of referring to off-site provisioning, or a new architecture for provisioning.

At the same time as SaaS entered the market, there was a strong buzz in terms of what was referred to as Cloud Computing. Cloud Computing (or Cloud, for short) initially developed as a new brand of grid computing, offering distributed computational resources packaged into a service, i.e. computing as a utility. The first commercial packaging of Cloud was introduced by Amazon through their Elastic Compute Cloud in 2006. These distributed resources were all owned by the Cloud vendor, and packaged in such a manner so the customer would not have to think about the underlying architecture or the changes in required processing power over time. Instead, we saw the birth of a model where organizations who previously had to invest in servers now could pay for computational power as they went along, with a dynamic sizing of the amount of servers that they had access to.

As with any radical new innovation related to IT, initial discussions about the implications of the said innovation were elevated. With this being a new service and market phenomenon rather than a new technology (grid computing and server virtualization), the adoption patterns were direct and substantial, with industry analysts pegging the compound annual growth rate for 2013 to around 25 percent. This constitutes a shift where organizations were previously building their own infrastructures to be able to handle the demands placed upon them by their own enterprise system installations, and now more and more are considering a shift to off-premise alternatives.

With Cloud constituting a radical new way of both distributing your computational needs and sourcing software, it is laden with a high level of difficulty in terms of clashes existing in dominant perspectives on what constitutes "professional IT" for an organization. Just sending everything up into something as ephemeral as a "Cloud" may not be acceptable, and hence there are multiple versions of clouds currently at play in the market. The traditional (or one might argue first wave) of Cloud constitutes what is referred to as "Private" clouds, where the using organization fully controls the computational resources and their governance. In contrast with this, we see the "Public" cloud where computational resources are not owned by the using firm, but rather shared. This includes the services of the previously mentioned Amazon AWS and Microsoft Azure. With firms having heterogeneous requirements in respect of their computational needs (different levels of security, jurisdictional aspects et cetera), these two types are often combined into a third type, i.e. the "Hybrid" cloud.

Albeit suffering from what Benders and Van Veen (2001) would refer to as "interpretative viability", Cloud is defined as consisting of four elements:

1 Software as a Service (SaaS)
2 Infrastructure as a Service (IaaS)
3 Network as a Service (NaaS)
4 Platform as a Service (PaaS)

Among these four, we have already addressed SaaS and we will consider IaaS and NaaS as being by large self-explanatory. As for PaaS, this has become a darling of the industry analysts over the years, with a high emphasis on expectations related to its future growth. One interpretation of PaaS is that it contains the development environment and necessary stack for building and deploying your own functionality into the cloud. Through this, it combines the IaaS, NaaS and SaaS categories, with an emphasis on what you need to build your own solutions through adaptations of existing solutions and the inclusion of new applications.

Platforms

We now introduce the notion of platforms through a recapitulation of the almost epic battle between Microsoft and Apple. During the last three decades, these two firms have been in direct competition on several markets with varying levels of success over time. By taking a closer look at some of their key releases in terms of features and success, we hope to add an initial understanding of what a platform actually is.

The battle between Microsoft and Apple started in the mid 1980s, and originates around the innovation of a graphical user interface (GUI) for computers. Previous interfaces required programming skills whereas the GUI opened the computer to an entirely new range of users. On November 20, 1985 Microsoft released their product Windows 1.0, the first operating system equipped with a GUI for personal computers.

By 1989, Apple introduced their take on the operating system (OS 5.0.4) taking the GUI to the next level. The product was well received and involved incremental innovation of the GUI. But it was not until the release of Windows 3 that things really started to take off for Microsoft. Windows 3 offered significantly enhanced support for software developers through the release of a Software development kit (SDK). The SDK encouraged writing programs, not device drivers as before. The result of this was that Microsoft was able to significantly out-perform Apple during the nineties and noughties in terms of market share and financial performance.

But in 2001, something radically different occurs. After a long tradition of being a closed system, Apple starts to open up to a new kind of structured interaction with their users. They do so through integrating the previously separate music industry into the Apple "package" by the release of the music player iPod, tightly connected to an online marketplace for music. The marketplace and the music player were also tightly connected to Apple computers and the Apple operating system. The users could purchase music, make and share playlists and rate content, differentiating the use of their Apple products from that offered by Microsoft.

From this point on, Apple continues to integrate new industries into their offering, expanding the scope of use for their products, with the most noticeable example being the introduction of the iPhone, a hybrid of a phone and a small computer (the first to be coined a Smart phone). By May 26, 2010 Apple surpasses Microsoft, becoming the highest-valued technology firm in the world.

So, how can a firm on the verge of bancruptcy in 1997 become the highest valued technology firm in the world over a period of only 15 years? The answer to this question lies in part in their application of a platform strategy and their shift towards delivering a platform and not a complete solution. In the next section, we will introduce a conceptual model and address the basic concepts, while at the same time elaborating on the answer to the question.

DEFINITION

Throughout the years, there have been numerous attempts at definitions related to platforms. In Table 2.1, we give a brief overview of a selection of these definitions.

Table 2.1 Overview of definitions of various types of platforms.

Type of platform	Definition	Source
Platform	"… a raised level surface on which people or things can stand, usually a discrete structure intended for a particular activity or operation"	Oxford English Dictionary
Software platform	"… the extensible codebase of a software-based system that provides core functionality shared by the modules that interoperate with it and interfaces through which they operate …"	Tiwana et al., 2010, p. 676
Product platform	"… a set of common components, modules, or parts from which a stream of derivative products can be efficiently created and launched"	Meyer and Lehnerd, 1997, p. 7
Supply Chain Platforms	"… a set of subsystems and interfaces that forms a common structure from which a stream of derivate products can be efficiently developed and produced by partners along a supply chain"	Gawer, 2009, p. 52
Platform product	Products that "meet the needs of a core group of customers but [are designed] for easy modifications into derivatives through addition, substitution, or removal of features"	Wheelwright and Clark, 1992, p. 73
Platform (economics)	Services, products, institutions or firms that mediate transaction between different groups of agents	Rochet and Tirole, 2003
Platform	"… the collection of assets that are shared by a set of products"	Robertson and Ulrich, 1998, p. 20
Platform (industry)	"… a bundle of standard components around which buyers and sellers coordinate efforts"	Bresnahan and Greenstein, 1999, p. 4
Platform-mediated network	"… is comprised of users whose interactions are subject to network effects, along with one or more intermediaries who organize a platform that facilitates users' interactions"	Eisenmann, Parker and Van Alstyne, 2011, p. 1272
Industry Platform	"… products, services or technologies that are developed by one or several firms, and that serve as foundations upon which other firms can build complementary products, services or technologies"	Gawer, 2009, p. 54

This vast plethora of definitions (as well as range of foci) perhaps only adds to the general notion of the field of platforms being highly complex. We will hence try to delimit our focus by offering our own take on how a platform is defined.

© STUDENTLITTERATUR

We define platform by expanding Meyer and Lehnerd (1997) with inspiration from Eisenmann, Parker and Van Alstyne (2011) as:

a package of common parts from which a stream of derivatives can be efficiently created and launched with network effects.

In this definition lies the delimitation away from delivering a complete product or service (i.e. solution), towards establishing control over the *market* for derivatives (see Figure 2.5). Derivatives refer to complementary products and/or services such as Apps and components that are not packaged together with the platform itself. In addition to this, the definition highlights the rationale behind the platform, i.e. the facilitation and exploitation of network effects. Examples of platforms fitting this definition include such diverse solutions such as PayPal, Amazon, Visa, Wii, Xbox360, IBM, Spotify, Salesforce and Facebook.

One of the core issues for why platform strategies are becoming more and more prevalent lies in the balance between achieving economies of scale and

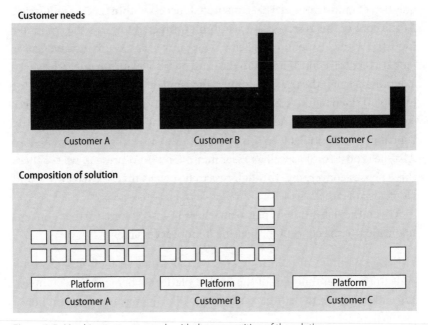

Figure 2.5 Matching customer needs with the composition of the solution.

scope. According to our definition of platform, the separation between the platform and the derivative products is in itself a safeguard for handling this trade-off. In terms of the platform, the platform owner can focus on a high level of robustness and efficiency, without this impacting negatively on the experience of the user in terms of evolutionary qualities. Matching the needs of a customer becomes easier if you delimit the scope of the core components, and shift the responsibility of adaptability and customer fit to a collection of derivative products. Hence, alignment or functional fit for a customer is achieved through combining the platform with available derivative products, effectively matching the fit between the needs and the composition of the solution, as presented in Figure 2.5.

According to Gawer (2011) we have seen the emergence of research into the business phenomenon of platforms as following three phases. First, we see research conducted within the field of product development, covering issues related to projects focused on new generations of products. This phase (see Wheelwright and Clark, 1992 or an introduction) was followed by a turn towards technology and industry. Here, researchers and technology strategists switched attention from the development of products to the question of industries and what constituted success within specific industries. At the core of this research, we see studies directed towards the computer industry, with Cusumano and Selby (1995) as well as Cusumano and Gawer (2002) as central contributions. In the third phase of platform research, we see a dominance of industrial economics, focusing on issues related to two- (or multiple-) sided markets studied through a variety of empirical perspectives such as the credit card industry, software and dating services. Noteworthy contributions attributable to this phase include the works of Parker and Van Alstyne (2005; 2010) as well as Eisenmann (2008). At present, we see these three phases converging, through research such as that of Ghazawhne and Henfridsson (2013).

Given the definition of platform, there is a need for a further conceptualization of the concept for making it more accessible.

Exhibit: The issue of revenue-sharing

In 2013, Jacobides and McDuffie published a comparison of how well platform owners have managed to control the value generated throughout the value chains. According to their findings, they see a sharp contrast between how the computer sector and the automobile sector has managed to control the sharing of revenue over time.

According to Jacobides and McDuffie (2013), the automobile sector has managed to control a much higher percentage of the total revenue generated over time, whereas the computer sector has experienced a steady decline in the share of total industry market cap. From computers initially (in 1978) being "complete solutions" as we have previously described, they have turned into platforms with externalized development of electrical components, software and services, with a sharing of revenues as a direct consequence. During the same time period we see widespread computerization, with a massive increase in the total amount of computers, whereas the automobile sector has had a more modest development. In contrast with the Jacobides and McDuffy, it might be relevant to look into the practice of revenue-sharing as one proxy for platform viability. This is something that we will return to later on in this chapter.

A CONCEPTUAL MODEL OF PLATFORMS

The work of creating a conceptual model of platforms was conducted during the spring of 2014, utilizing a combination of previous research and experience from trying to communicate the function of platforms, both in the facility of consultants and teachers.

The results of this process can be seen in Figure 2.6 (on the next page), and we will devote some time to expanding on the content and function of each element in the conceptual model.

Stakeholders: Owner, Innovator and User

As seen in the model, the stakeholders of the platform are divided into three categories based on their function. The Owner constitutes the actor involved in sponsoring and facilitating the interchange between Innovator

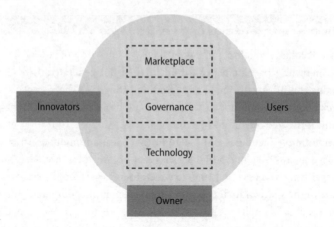

Figure 2.6 Conceptual model of platforms.

and User. In terms of previously described platforms, this would be the Googles, Intels, Apples and Salesforces of the world. In contrast with earlier conceptions of the platform owner, we avoid making the distinction between platform owner and platform sponsor (as seen in the works of van Alstyne and associates), with the rationale of simplification and the avoidance of unnecessary complexity.

Choosing to refer to this actor as an "Owner" does, however, invite the discussion of what it actually is that is "owned". The Owner does not (necessarily) own the derivatives traded on the platform. They do, on the other hand, own the transactions made on the platform, i.e. the monetary and IP-related traffic facilitated by the platform. The Owner is often the initiator of the initiatives underlying the platform. They are the actors most involved in the design and construction of the business model and governance of the platform. From this perspective, they are the owners of the processes, structures and relational mechanisms that constitute the governance of the platform, controlling both what derivatives are made possible, and which derivatives are sold.

In terms of the Innovator, this refers to the group of stakeholders involved with the design, realization and marketing of derivatives. In most cases these are independent, third party organizations and/or individuals, but they may also be associated with the Owner in partnerships et cetera. With some Owners controlling the platform through more or less closed means of association such as quality assurance, partnership structures et cetera, the number of Innovators is contingent on the openness of the platform. The rationale for Innovators joining the platform ranges from the opportunistic to the strategic, depending on the individual Innovator and the platform in question.

The User constitutes the third and final category of stakeholders. These (individuals and/or organizations) take part in the creation of value in the platform through purchasing and/or using the derivatives. In some cases this use also involves feedback in the form of reviews and ratings. The rationale for joining the platform lies in the access to superior functionality through the derivatives and/or path dependencies such as having previously invested in the platform (or nucleus of the platform) and now perceiving the switching costs as insurmountable.

In addition to the stakeholders, the platform also consists of three elements of content, which we will address in the section below.

Content: Technology, Governance and Marketplace

In terms of the content of the platform, as we refer to it in this book, there are three elements.

First, we have the element of technology. With the platform being dependent upon an underlying structure in some form (here referred to as "Technology"), the element of technology consists of a core, interfaces and an installed base.

In terms of the *core*, this is perceived as the underlying foundational architecture and technologies upon which both use and additional development of derivatives is contingent. We see the core as the basic structure, the assumptions of use and utility, and the non-exclusive components that together constitute the backbone of the platform offering and the core functionality.

Interfaces refer to the standardized means through which derivatives access and utilize the core functionality. In software, this is manifested in both the architectural guidelines for integration (e.g. SOA) and the functional specifications for the said integration (e.g. APIs). The interfaces allow for what Nicholas Luhmann (1995) refers to as "functional simplification", and economic rationale in the development of derivatives.

As for the *installed base*, this is used as a complement and expansion of market share in order to describe the platform's existence over time. It refers to the instances of the platform (or previous versions of the core) currently in use. In the case of enterprise systems, this would refer to both on-site and cloud-based installations with previous versions of the enterprise system. Previous conceptual models of platforms have failed to address this aspect of technology, but with platforms becoming more and more prevalent in the market, we believe that this needs be taken into consideration.

The installed base of current and previous versions of the platforms introduces the notion of time into the equation. This is perhaps most relevant for non-consumer oriented software technologies such as enterprise systems, where the time between upgrades varies substantially and the management of different versions of software is a difficult issue. From the perspective of the Owner, this puts an emphasis on slow growth in terms of core functionality, and the necessity for strong control over the available interfaces. Hence, it brings with it a "strangulation of possibilities", as expressed by one platform owner we interviewed.

Second, a platform contains the element of Governance, stipulating the *business rules* regarding how to act and interact on the platform. The rules include how to buy, add and edit derivatives, and how to provide feedback and experiences from usage. Furthermore, Governance includes how to make derivatives visible to others, and *legal requirements* regarding support and responsibilities for usage. Governance also stipulates *membership* aspects on the platform and other legal issues. Rules are defined so as to make business scalable, i.e. that it should require a minimum of human interaction and instead focus on automated business processes. In order to automate business processes, legal requirements must be fulfilled such as the terms of responsibility for each respective content component. Each stakeholder must accept and conform to all the rules, and it is not possible to treat stakeholders individually and make exceptions.

Third, we have the element of Marketplace. In accordance with Callon's critique of the concept of Market (see Exhibit on the next page), the marketplace refers to the physical and/or logical space that facilitates the exchange of derivatives. A platform has at least two marketplaces. One marketplace is directed towards the User of the platform, the other marketplace is directed towards Innovator. The marketplace directed towards

Exhibit: Callon's critique and Multisided markets

The French sociologist Michel Callon (1998, p. 1) notes that albeit being a cornerstone and central institution in the field of economics, the concept of the Market is sadly underdeveloped.

> While the market denotes the abstract mechanisms whereby supply and demand confront each other and adjust themselves in search of a compromise, the marketplace is far closer to ordinary experience and refers to the place in which exchange occurs.

Following this line of thought, he concludes that there is a shortcoming in economic theory, and that this shortcoming is related to the lack of interest shown in the marketplace. Regardless of this alleged shortcoming in economic theory, a substantial amount of interest has been devoted to better understanding of what is referred to as "Multi-sided Markets".

These markets, be that in the form of internet-facilitated platforms such as eBay, Visa or Linux, are described as mediators between actors, i.e. markets facing not one but several actors. Looking more closely into one example of such a market (Google's Android platform), we can identify at least five sides. First you have the cellphone manufacturers that OEM their products, including the operating system into their handheld devices, and opening up their phones to the large assortment of apps available through Android. Second, you have the third-party Innovators of apps, which gain access to a market for their products and/ or services. Third, you have media buyers that utilize the platform as a basis for marketing. Fourth, you have the telephone operators, bundling their services with special offers for handheld devices. Fifth and perhaps finally, you have the users of the bundle of services and products manifested in the handheld device.

The beauty in this perspective on something as (arguably) simple as a phone lies in the ability to address different takes on the value exchanges taking place through the platform. Each side of the market can be equipped with its own set of logic, revenue streams and value generation, yet at the same time they all work together in creating a complete solution for the involved parties. As previously noted, this perspective on platforms could be seen as constituting a third phase of research into platforms.

the User (*sales environment*) promotes derivatives, and communicates the experiences from other users regarding the said derivatives. The marketplace directed towards the Innovator promotes an attractive *development environment* and access to the market of Users.

Core concepts

Cocreation

The reason for the industrial trend towards platforms is not motivated by technical innovation, but rather the classic economic rationale of increased efficiency and effectiveness.

It is no longer possible for the single vendor to provide a complete solution meeting "all needs"; it is also not efficient to have specific one-to-one solutions for solving additional requests that may have a significant larger potential market.

Through a platform approach, the enterprise system provider may facilitate a meeting between providers and users that concerns a scope outside the enterprise system, but building on information and infrastructure from the enterprise system. The platform approach significantly increases the reuse of enterprise system adaptations, and opens up for a close collaboration between system Owners, system Innovators and system Users.

From the user's perspective, it is valuable to share costs for developing niche components with others; for the Innovators it is valuable to sell the same component to more than one customer (the boundary between service and product is blurring), and for the provider it is valuable to have additional functionality developed on top of the platform. Value is *cocreated* via collaboration between the actors. Through collaboration, a critical mass of adaptations and niche functionality may be reached that facilitates diverse market needs.

Successful platforms experience non-linear value creation increase in relation to the number of stakeholders involved; thus "good" content increases the overall gravity and attractiveness of the platform and the surrounding innovation system thanks to the power of cocreation.

Openness

The platform owner decides what aspects of the platform are to remain open for partner adaptations and integration, and what parts should remain closed (the core). The level of platform openness directly dictates the innovation domain for the platform Innovators. In this sense, the level of openness is also a key variable for how attractive the platform is in the eyes of the Innovators. A platform that is too closed will choke the innovation, and a platform that is too open will not guide the innovative power of the Innovators in the "right" direction from a market demand perspective.

Exhibit: Why does openness work?

It is easy to have an intuitive understanding of the value from openness for the platform owner, but how does it translate to economics?

In order to understand this, we need to compare openness with the alternative, not being open and then compare. In a closed platform, the Owner takes care of everything and sells a ready solution.

In an open platform, the platform owner gives part of the potential value from the platform to an innovator.

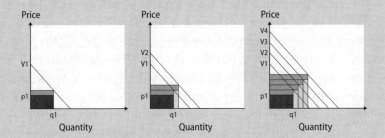

Figure 2.7 Why does Openness work?

The innovator adds new layers of value reaching additional, new customers.

The Platform owner increases sales and saves costs, and the Innovator gets access to a market. As this simple logic is scaled, the platform Owner receives substantial value from the Innovator's derivatives.

The challenge for the platform owner is to design the platform so that the "right" variables and features are open, and that the rest is put in an attractive package.

Competition

Many businesses are attracted by the "platform promise" of exceptional value creation by merely providing "something clever" between producers and users. There are many ongoing *battles* between platforms. Platform users will end up choosing one or on rare occasions two providers of the same platform type. Examples of IT-related platform battlegrounds are Game consoles (Xbox, Wii, Playstation), Computer OS (Windows, MacOS, Unix), Smartphone (iOS, Android, Windows phone), Search (Google, Bing), Switches (Cisco, IBM, HP) and Social networks (Facebook, Twitter, LinkedIn).

Worth mentioning is also some of the failed platforms such as BETA and Laserdisc for watching recorded video content, the Atari game console, the Symbian operating system for mobile phones, Altavista and Ask Jeeves for web search, to name a few.

The outcome of platform battles are difficult to predict; simply betting on the "best" product or the "deepest pockets" will not pick the winner. A majority of the platform-related activities (and value creation) is done outside the organizational border of the platform owner, and the platform's attractiveness and value creation is also done beyond the control of the platform owner. Platform battle success will depend on the innovation capacity of the ecosystem of partners surrounding the platform and their willingness and capability to innovate based on the platform offer. As you can see, platform battles are directly related to the level of cocreation.

Platform Strategies

During the past decade, there have been several attempts from companies attempting to formulate and implement a platform *strategy*. Platform scholars such as Gawer and Cusumano have studied platform leaders and platform leader wannabes extensively (Gawer and Cusumano, 2008). Their key findings are presented regarding a few selected strategic concepts.

Incompatible, competing standards are not platforms, but an under-

Exhibit: Standards Wars

In a 1999 article in the *California Management Review*, Shapiro and Varian coined the term standards wars as "...battles for market dominance between incompatible technologies..." (p.8). Written around the time of the battle between Microsoft and Netscape for dominance over the web browser, the article identifies generic strategies employed for waging standard wars.

As noted by the authors, standards wars are of particular interest (and hence particularly bitter...) in markets with strong network effects derived from compatibility. With customers aspiring for network effects and combinatory effects of different technologies, the vendors (or alliances) are pushed towards drastic measures in order to ascertain their continued existence.

According to Shapiro and Varian, there are seven key assets that will determine a vendor's success in waging a standards war. These include control over an installed base of users, the ability to innovate, acquiring first-mover advantages and strength in derivatives.

In addition to this, they offer five tips for firms preparing for a standards war.

1 Assemble allies. Strength is in numbers, so make sure that you do not delimit your search for allies.
2 Use pre-emptive tactics. Use rapid design cycles, quick deals with important customers and penetration pricing.
3 Manage your customers' expectations, in order to convince both your customers and the Innovators of derivatives that you will win the war. Aggressive marketing, early announcements and visible commitments.
4 Once the war is won, don't rest. Make your solution attractive to new customers and don't be overly fixated with backward compatibility.
5 Avoid survival pricing. If you fall behind in the standards war, avoid signaling weakness. In this case it is advisable to focus on interoperability with the leading standard.

standing of how standards competition is likely to play out is an important part of understanding which platform is likely to become dominant (Cusamou, 2010). There is an important distinction between a product platform and an industry platform. A product platform is to a large extent under the control of one company, whereas an industry platform is comprised of a critical technology core that others build on top of. The "others" make up an innovation ecosystem that resides outside the jurisdictional boundaries of the platform provider and thus outside the formal control of the platform provider. It is common that strategic confusion arises regarding what kind of platform strategy a company is perusing (platform or product), and this leads to unfortunate results.

A company aspiring to maintain or take a leading platform role must formulate a clear strategy to do so. There are two strategic phases that must be successfully executed in order to establish an industry-leading platform, they are called Coring and Tipping (Ibid). During the Coring phase, a company identifies and designs a technical component that is fundamental to a technological system and market. The component may be referred to as core if it resolves problems related to a large population of the system.

> Coming up with platform-like technologies may well be easier than coming up with business strategies that encourage partners and customers to adopt a particular technology.
>
> GAWER & CUSUMANO, 2008, P. 3

As expressed by Gawer and Cusumano, it is usually not the technical aspects of the platform initiative that is most challenging; the challenge resides in the business- and strategic issues. There must be clear value-related incentives for platform partners for why they should build and contribute on top of the platform. The value of the platform is directly related to the aggregation of the core, the components and the capacity for recurring innovations, cocreation.

In a platform battle where two companies compete for the position of platform leader, there are a few things you can do to "tip" the outcome in your favor, and this strategy is called Tipping. A tipping strategy includes:

- Gain control over installed base
- Build brand equity
- Build manufacturing, distribution and service capabilities
- Play with price on different sides of the multi-sided market; free/ fee etc

The most extreme example of a tipping strategy is when a platform absorbs another market, and this is called *Platform envelopment* and is used to gain synergies from combining two or more networks. As an example, Google started out as a provider of a web search engine. But it was not until Google combined web search with enveloping the advertising industry that they became platform leaders. Previous "Internet companies" had been successful in attracting many users, but failed to convert this into a revenue-generating business; Google solved this by combining advertisement spaces in combination with "free" slots for presenting web search results. This is a good example of a successful implementation of a tipping strategy.

Economic rationale

So let us go back to the initial question at the beginning of this chapter: How is it possible for a company on the verge of bankruptcy (Apple) fifteen years ago to become one of the largest and most profitable IT company in the world today?

The answer lies in the way Apple combined the power of a multi-sided market with the integration of previously separated industries. Apple's core offering started out in hardware and operating systems, but in order to attract users and attention, Apple started adding user context, i.e. applications. They started out with administrative- and graphical tools for consumer- and corporate users. So far, they were in the same "game" as other computer companies, and they were not winning.

The game-changer came with Apple's introduction of the iPod and iTunes, a closed concept for selling, distributing, buying and recommending music. But the iPod and iTunes were not treated as separate businesses; instead they were integrated in Apple's core offering of computers. By combining the two (previously separated) markets, Apple could enjoy what is referred to as *network effects* (or *network externalities*, see Exhibit). Customers and content producers from one market fueled the other market, and vice versa. In other words, Apple created a platform that facilitated network effects.

After the success of the iPod and iTunes, Apple had the recipe for a scalable business model. They have used this recipe repeatedly on new markets (such as the reading tablet) and established markets (such as the telecommunication/ mobile phone). Each new market is integrated into the

Exhibit: The long tail

In the highly influential article "The Long Tail", the chief editor of Wired, Chris Anderson, wrote about the effects of new technology in the entertainment industry. According to Anderson, the current market suffers from a misconception in terms of the underlying assumption that revenue is achieved through economies of scale alone. Through contrasting the sales of physical retailers such as Barnes and Noble, Wal-Mart and Blockbuster with that of digital actors such as Rhapsody, Amazon and Netflix, Anderson shows that the physical retailers cater merely to the most popular items. This disregards the scattered needs of the many for niche markets in the spirit of Pareto efficiency.

This previously untapped market for not generally popular items is described as the Long Tail, a term borrowed from statistics and referring to a probability distribution with the majority of occurrences residing outside of the normal distribution. Given the Digitalization of Everything, the cost for distribution is diminished, for the first time making it possible to actually tap into this previously overlooked market. Or in the words of Anderson (2004, p. 8):

> This is the world of scarcity. Now with online distribution and retail, we are entering a world of abundance.

In line with this observation, Anderson offers advice on how to approach this long tail market:

1 Make everything readily available
   - Embrace niches
   - Aggregate dispersed audiences
   - It's more expensive to evaluate than to release
2 Cut the price in half, then lower it
   - Set price according to digital costs, not physical
   - It is possible to compete with freemium
3 Help me find it
   - Hits still matter
   - Use recommendations to drive demand down the Long Tail

Apple platform to further enhance the network effects. Apple has hence been achieving competitive advantages through superior network effects, not through superior stand-alone products. Apple has been winning due to a better platform strategy.

In addition to network effects it is important to understand how to get the pricing right on platforms with multi-sided markets. When done right, the pricing strategy fuels the growth of demand from both (multiple) market sides. Let us take the video game industry as an example. When Innovators develop games for the Microsoft Xbox, the Xbox platform receives additional content and becomes more attractive for players. When more players start using the Xbox platform, it becomes more attractive for Innovators to distribute their games on (Eisenmann et al. 2006).

It is also common to subsidize one side of the market and charge a premium for the other market side. Adobe is an example of using a subsidized pricing strategy: their .pdf Acrobat Reader is free but their solution to create .pdf documents has a significant fee.

In terms of the platform owner being dependent upon third-party development, one of the core issues lies in balancing what should be part of the platform and what should not.

The attractiveness of a platform is determined by several factors, the most important being openness. The platform may have a varying degree of openness in terms of technology (languages, standards and integration), business (rules, rights and responsibilities) and market (pricing, visibility and competition). A successful platform attracts a critical mass of content providers' continuously building on top of (and adding value to) the platform, meeting the needs of a critical mass of users. In other words, the success of the platform itself is directly contingent upon the existence of an ecosystem of actors adding value to the consumers of services through the platform. Thus, a lively innovation ecosystem surrounds successful platforms, creating value to all stakeholders involved.

ENTERPRISE SYSTEM PLATFORMS

Having devoted time to defining and describing the emergence of both enterprise systems and platforms, we will now address the concept of Enterprise System Platforms. With platforms in the technological sense of the word having been used for a long time within the enterprise systems market, we will present an alternative perspective, building on our previous definition of platforms. The purpose of this is to show how enterprise systems are emerging into *Enterprise System Platforms*, and what consequences this has for a student of enterprise systems.

Definition

We define Enterprise System Platform as:

> A set of common parts for standardized, enterprise-wide provision of information systems offered by a single vendor, including a stream of derivatives developed by complementary actors.

In terms of the conceptual model of platforms presented earlier, the very nature of the enterprise system market with a separation of developing and consulting firms is handled through perceiving the consulting activities as happening outside of the platform itself. These are adjacent activities related to the platform, but not transactions handled through it. Hence, the stakeholder category of Innovator contains both organizations working with the marketing of derivatives and the actual development of derivatives. In many cases these are the same type of firms, and in other cases they are different types.

The Turn to Platforms in Enterprise Systems

As previously noted, the general trend for firms acting within the IT industry has been to move towards a platform logic (Gawer and Cusumano, 2002). This can be seen in relation to the wide-scale success of Apple's iOS and the massive onslaught of apps and associated Innovators. From a production perspective, this can be understood as the externalization of production, i.e. a form of outsourcing of development. What sets this aside from regular outsourcing is, however, the distribution of risk. Through employing platform strategies by the use of app stores, we see that the platform owners can lower their business risk associated with developing added functionality and niche customizations. Instead, they externalize this development to third-party Innovators, and focus their efforts on maintaining the platform.

The first real example of this type of strategy we saw in the market for enterprise systems was when Salesforce, the CRM vendor, initiated their AppExchange initiative in 2005. Previously, they had sold standardized CRM solutions as-a-service, but through force.com they did two simultaneous things. First, they increased the level of openness in regard to Innovators, so that people on the outside of the organization could start to use Salesforce as a development environment. Second, they introduced the possibility for third-party Innovators to market and sell their added functionality and customizations (packaged as apps) through a marketplace. Hence, they provided the means and the incentive for externalized development. By 2009, they launched their force.com product, officially moving towards delivering Platform as a Service (PaaS). Today (2014), they have over 2,000 apps with a total of over 2 million installs.

Exhibit: Vendor strategies towards SaaS

At the same time as Salesforce was moving towards PaaS, the other main vendors were still struggling to deliver pure-play SaaS solutions. In a research project conducted between 2008–2011 (Magnusson, Juell-Skielse, Enquist & Uppström, 2012), we studied this transition, and noticed a sharp contrast between enterprise systems vendors founded before and after the widespread adoption of SOA. For the incumbent vendors, the level of complexity made any delivery of pure SaaS highly complex from both a technical and business related perspective. From a technical perspective, they were well adapted towards providing their solutions through the Cloud, yet the decomposition of their products into smaller chunks made all other packaging than the traditional monolith solution difficult. This was not solely related to the packaging and marketing being new, but also to issues such as incentive schemes for the sales staff and cash flow. With the organizations being used to selling complete solutions and receiving a large portion of the revenue up front, they were now facing a more risky and monthly cash flow. In summarizing the project, we found that the primary challenge for incumbent firms with moving towards SaaS packaging and delivery was found in issues related to finance, not technology.

By 2012, the powerful industry analysts such as Gartner and Forrester started to push the envelope in terms of why software vendors needed to consider the move towards PaaS instead of (or from) SaaS. With the success of Salesforce to some extent and Apple's iOS to a larger extent, a selection of platforms had started to dominate the market for consumerized IT, and the market for enterprise systems had as of yet not seen any substantial movement (apart from NetSuite). Following this turn, we can look at the enterprise systems market from the perspective of different business models. We have simplified the differentiation between different business models along two axes, one being the internalization versus externalization of development, and the other being the offering of services or products.

As seen in Figure 2.8, the Monolith business model involves the delivery of a product and internal development. Vendors such as Sweden's IFS, Intentia (currently iFor) and IBS all subscribed to this model during the early noughties. This involved taking control over the entire business opportunity, with consulting, customization, development and sales. In times of prosperity, this model works well, but as they found out during the first decade of the 21st century, it was not optimal for situations where the market fluctuated along with demand.

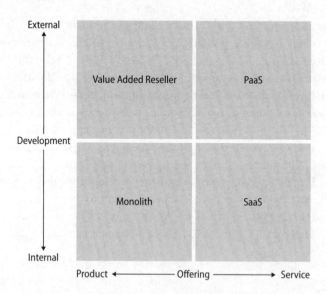

Figure 2.8 Adopted from Ladhe, Magnusson & Nilsson (2013).

The larger international vendors such as SAP and Microsoft utilized a different model, with externalization of sales, consulting and customization to partner firms. This model, described in the matrix as Value Added Reseller (VAR), proved to be superior in terms of managing fluctuations in demand. Instead of having to acquire the competence needed for selling and consulting in relation to the enterprise system, they focused on attracting partners such as Accenture, Bearing Point et cetera and shared the spoils with them.

In the mid noughties, a new model for the packaging and provisioning of software started to emerge. As previously described, Software as a Service (SaaS) started to gain momentum, mainly through challenging vendors that from the start had this as a model for delivery. Instead of having to attract competence and build an organization for sales and consulting (such as in the case of the Monolith) or to form partnerships (such as in the case of the VAR), these vendors avoided these thresholds and sold directly through the Internet. Their solutions were tailored to attract the end-users through offering a limited amount of functionality, such as CRM in the case of Salesforce, with the cost per user being low enough to pass "under the radar" of corporate attention, i.e. Shadow IT (see Chapter 2, Investments and the Investment context).

In many of the cases we studied throughout this period in time, we saw that the incumbent vendors were taken aback by the speed and veracity with which these vendors attained market shares. Hence, the incumbent vendors saw it necessary to adapt their business models to the sign of the times, or in other words re-packaging their previously on-site installation-based delivery models towards offering their products as services, often on a subscription basis. Unfortunately for the vendors applying a VAR business model, they were faced with the difficulty of competing against vendors that required very little consulting assistance (hence making their existing partnerships less lucrative), while at the same time having to reframe their previous product offerings to a smaller scope. Very few of the firms that we studied were able to make this transition, and ended up with a hybrid logic of packaging their offering as SaaS but delivering it according to their previous models.

The last stage of these developments started to occur in parallel with the shift towards SaaS in the late noughties. With the challenging vendors starting to understand the merits of a limited scoped SaaS, accepting the disintegration of monolith systems into a collection of services with low-cost integration through standardized interoperability, they started to look for alternative avenues for driving revenue. With limited organizations, solely focused on developing their core product, they were not in a position where they wanted to compete head-on with the incumbent vendors. Instead, they utilized the lessons learned from platform business models such as that of Apple. This involved externalization of development of complementary functionality, making it possible for others to take the business risk for developing niche functionality.

The way they handled this was through first creating a development environment where the APIs of the enterprise system were selectively made open to derivative services. At the same time, they utilized their market presence to attract third-party Innovators under the rationale that these would be given access to their entire customer base. This development environment had two main purposes: both to attract a new set of "free" resources through opening up their original product, and to delimit the range of what was technologically possible to develop. This delimitation was designed to avoid integration mishaps and a potential diminishing of quality as experienced by the end-user. In other words, the development environment both opened and closed the development process. The last step was to create a market environment or "app store" where the end-user could explore and purchase the derivatives, i.e. driving revenue for both the enterprise system vendor and the third-party Innovator.

Through these steps, challenging vendors started to move from following a SaaS business model to that of PaaS.

Consequences of the Turn to Platforms

The consequences of more and more enterprise system vendors moving towards the PaaS business model, or as in the case of the incumbent vendors adding this business model to their plethora of previous business models, are substantial for all involved parties. As previously noted, the vendors exist in an eco system with partners, both in the form of consultants and third-party Innovators, and customers. The platform business model implies the externalization of development of derivatives, but at the same time its consumerized offering threatens to delimit the previous revenue streams

Exhibit: Cloud Services Brokerage

In 2009, we proposed that a large ERP consulting firm should consider changing their business model in a radical fashion. Instead of attending to their customers' needs in helping them to choose and implement ERP systems, they should consider taking on the role of what we referred to as "Service brokers".

With the consulting firm having developed and utilized their own standardized process model for years, they were in a position where they had understood the linkages between processes and a selection of leading ERP solutions on the market. With this as structural capital, we proposed that they should move towards establishing their own GUI through Microsoft Sharepoint, and create web parts for each "service" executed by ERP systems. With this in place, they could configure the business processes together with the customers, and then "simply" add functionality from the selection of several ERPs best suited for the task at this particular period in time.

What we proposed was a radical shift from simply helping customers procure a single ERP system towards a continuous, pluralistic provisioning fitting the changing demands of the customer over time. The system park of a single firm would hence change over time, as the preferences of the organization changed, striving for a perfect fit between needs and functionality.

In more recent years, this concept of service brokerage has been highlighted by industry analysts such as Gartner and Forrester as the next frontier in cloud computing. With the disintegration of systems, with ERP systems becoming provisioned as bundles of services, there is a business opportunity for consulting firms with knowledge of processes and services. Brokering the services from both public and private clouds either through aggregation, integration or customization would be a valuable added value to the market. This phenomenon is now referred to as "Cloud Services Brokerage" and we expect it to become even more popular as cloud computing continues to be adopted and the disintegration of systems continues. In the backwater of this development, utility process outsourcing will offer another avenue of expansion.

associated with consulting, a key motivation for partner organizations to invest in knowledge and know-how in individual enterprise systems.

Several researchers have pointed out the disruptive potential of this development for professions such as that of consultants. With consultants previously being the direct link between the enterprise system vendor and the customers, offering sales and the support for operationalization and realization of benefits associated with the enterprise system investment, we are now experiencing a potential marginalization of the consultants. This is, according to Christensen, Wang and Van Bever (2013), a development that we currently see the first signs of. From previously having full control over the customer (or clients), the consulting firms are more and more losing ground. The reason behind this lies in the commoditization of IT, something that we see as a direct consequence of the turn to platforms as previously described.

With customizations (previously a lucrative business for the consultants) more and more becoming a commodity, packaged as derivatives and sold through the enterprise system app store, they are losing much of their previous raison d'être. If the "appification" of customizations and added functionality continues, as we expect it will, these firms need to find alternative avenues of revenue. This in turn creates a position where the vendors subscribing to the VAR business model are left without support from the firms normally adding value and selling their solutions. If there is no profit to be made in selling (since customers make one large, i.e. platform choice, and then numerous decentralized procurements through the associated app store), they will cease selling and the vendor will more and more have to turn towards the Monolith business model, having their own sales staff at hand. If there is no profit to be made in consulting (since standardization and interoperability has diminished the need for adapting software, and shifted this towards the selection of services which is controlled by the customers themselves or a Cloud Services Brokerage firm), they will cease consulting and the vendor will be left in a position where competence needs to be internalized.

Hence, we acknowledge the potential disruptive nature of PaaS for the enterprise system market. On the other hand, there are multiple potential up-sides to the turn to services as well. As we described earlier, the platform brings with it the promise of avoiding the trade-off between economies of scale and economies of scope. The reason for this lies in the very basis of the "app" or "service" as an atom, and we will devote some time to explaining this in more detail.

In the introduction of this book, we discussed the notion of a dis-integration of the whole into smaller parts. This "whole" in terms of the enterprise system moving towards a platform logic is the packaged software itself. From previously being large (if not enormous) in scope, the turn to platforms involves a delimitation of scope and a retreat from the idea of complete solutions. Focusing on the platform, and mediating the contact between third-party development and customer end-use, the vendor can focus on the core functionality needed to facilitate externalized development and brokering the exchanges.

This activity is, however, not a retreat from expanding the components constituting the platform. As seen in examples such as Microsoft and their inclusion of the Explorer Internet browser, or Apple and their inclusion of previous apps into the iOS, basic functionality is plastic and changes over time. Hence, vendors turning to the platform logic need to constantly consider the boundaries of the core vis á vis the derivatives. When use of specific functionality previously delivered as derivatives increases, it may reach a level where it should be considered for inclusion.

Albeit a central activity for any platform owner, this activity has not been studied sufficiently in the empirical realm. There are several case studies of inclusions, yet we see few examples of studies that problematize the activity sufficiently. One way of looking at this would be to equate the inclusion of derivatives into the core as "bloating", previously described as the central strategy during the adolescence of enterprise systems. Expanding the core results in a potential decrease in agility, and if left unchecked may risk returning us to a situation where the scope of systems got out of hand. Hence, additional studies of exclusions are warranted, but we have yet to see any examples of this.

Turning our attention to the consequences for the end users or customers of the Enterprise System Platform, the developments described in this book paint a much brighter picture. With the central issues facing organizations today being related to balancing control over the IT environment (geared towards economies of scale), while at the same time tapping into the benefits of user-driven innovation and proactivity (geared towards economies of scope), platforms seem to be ideally suited. With an ample supply of derivatives, ready to be seamlessly integrated and immediately used, combinatory rather than customized benefits seem to be on the cusp of the possible. This is, however, contingent on two factors that we will discuss in brief: platform viability and inter-platform operability.

In terms of *platform viability*, this refers to the long-term capability of the platform to attract and attain a critical mass of Innovators and users. As previously noted, a platform with insufficient gravitational pull will result in sub-par network effects and a lack of rationale. In other words, without the critical mass being reached, the platform will not add sufficient value to be able to compete for market attention. Some examples exist where subsidizing and ample funding will be able to keep the platform going for some time, yet without the network effects the platform will sooner or later run the risk of implosion.

Measuring platform viability is hence associated with substantial difficulties. Adding the time dimension to any assessment in order to predict future value is of course difficult, but there are some indicators that may be of service for an assessment of platform viability. The first is that of financial stability of the platform owner. Here, we see that examples of successful platforms without substantial financial backing are highly rare. Even in examples such as the Swedish consumer-oriented platform Spotify, substantial funding was necessary and even today continually poses a threat for viability. The second indicator of platform viability is the total amount of derivatives attained through the platform. Here, we see two possible measures. One is the total amount of downloads, which can be used as an indication of the current potential value of joining the platform. This is,

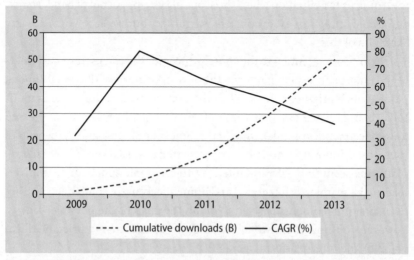

Figure 2.9 CAGR and Cumulative downloaded apps iOS (2009–2013), source Statista.com

however, interesting from a historic perspective, not directly applicable as an indication of the future performance of the platform. Instead, we can look at the Compound Annual Growth Rate (CAGR) of derivatives. In Figure 2.9 we have used statistics from Statista.com on the total amount of available apps for iOS (with this being perceived as a platform), as an illustration.

In terms of the cumulative downloads, we see a staggering 50 billion being reached by 2013, with an apparently stable increase over time. Looking at the CAGR we see that since 2010 there has been a continuous drop in relative growth by 50 percent up to 2013. Hence, using CAGR as an indicator for platform viability will lead us to the conclusion that after reaching critical mass, activity is now readily decreasing, perhaps as a result of customers being fed up, moving away towards alternative platforms.

With the cumulative downloads as an indicator of consumer demand, we can add the perspective of the total amount of available apps and its CAGR. Albeit being an indicator dependent upon a certain level of app turnover, we can use this to assess the attractiveness of the platform from the Innovators' perspective, i.e. the supply side. Here, once again we use the example of Apple iOS, looking at the total amount of available apps and the CAGR, as seen in Figure 2.10.

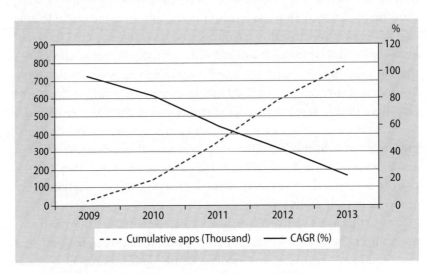

Figure 2.10 CAGR and Cumulative available apps iOS (2009–2013), source About.com (January used as a measure of the year).

This paints an even bleaker picture than the demand, with the CAGR dropping from a staggering nearly 100 percent in 2009 to below 30 percent in 2013. This also indicates that with the critical mass having been reached, there is a decrease in growth rate for the platform, i.e. it is slowing down or perhaps stabilizing. To this day there has been a lack of empirical research focused on the "autumn" phase of platform existence.

In terms of *inter-platform operability*, this refers to the capability of cross-platform development and use. We have previously addressed issues related to lock-in effects championed by the enterprise system vendors. With the ultimate goal of securing long-term profitability, they have traditionally been adamant in allowing loose coupling between the services offered through the enterprise system and the services offered by other systems and/or vendors. This technologically induced lock-in has, however, decreased during the past decade, and today we see an entirely different array of possibilities for the customers to multi-source their enterprise systems provision.

Turning our attention towards the hand-held devices and the platforms available for mobile use, the example of native apps versus HTML5 based apps is an illustrating example of how platform owners strive to avoid inter-platform operability. When HTML5 was launched and started to make a name for itself as the new standard for web development, the existing platform owners took an active stance towards delimiting the available APIs and subsequent functionality from the handhelds (such as GPS tracking, gyroscope et cetera) so that it would only be available for native apps. Since the platform owners' scope of control is limited to apps developed in the development environment and sold through the provisioning environment (app store in this case), they run the risk of losing control over both the installed base and the quality assurance, and subsequently the users' experience of their products (the hand-held ones themselves). With more and more apps being developed as HTML5 based web pages, they run the risk of losing both the revenues attributed to the sales of apps and the quality of service in their products.

From the users' perspective, the direct benefits of inter-platform operability is, however, overwhelmingly positive. With development moving more and more towards interoperability, we are rapidly approaching a time where the user has a hard time understanding why a certain set of services should not be available in their platform. Hence, inter-platform inoperability becomes a negative thing, and something that will result in platforms being discarded by the users. From an open innovation perspective, this results in platform-independent development of derivatives where the entire bulk of third-party Innovators could be focused on supporting multiple platforms with their creativity and work. In terms of the rate of diffusion of innovations, this would lead to a decrease in lag between conception, inception and critical mass being reached.

One early illustration of this can be seen in the previously discussed strategy of "platform envelopment" as proposed by Eisenmann, Parker and Van Alstyne (2007). When one platform owner moves into another platform owner's market, a multi-platform bundle becomes possible. One example of this would be for a smaller, full scale ERP vendor to repackage a limited part of their offering as an app to be sold as a derivative of a global CRM platform vendor's offering. For many ERP vendors this would be unthinkable, since they perceive the CRM system as a limited functionality within the ERP system, and not vice versa. But consider the CRM vendor having an excess of 200 thousand customers on a global level, and the ERP vendor being restricted to a local market with a total size of 2,000 customers.

Consider if the ERP vendor would for instance take their finance and controlling functionality, package this into an offering for, let us say the independent taxi companies, how would this impact their potential market? With the CRM vendor not considering finance and controlling as part of their core offering, they would be hard pressed for not allowing the ERP vendor to become a third-party Innovator, marketing their niche service to the CRM vendor's customer base. After all, it adds value to the customers, and offers close to zero competition. This is one example of how platform envelopment could be used to achieve increased sales, while at the same time driving inter-platform operability.

Both platform viability and inter-platform interoperability will be two important factors that influence the long-term success of platform strategies within enterprise systems.

Investments

INVESTING IN IT

With the enterprise systems being the hallmark of massive investments during the 1990s, the issue of how the organization should manage and govern IT quickly became a hot topic. During the early 1990s, investments in IT constituted more than 50 percent of all corporate capital investments. With this came a strong debate in terms of how we should regard the resource of IT, a debate that reached its pivotal moment in the early 2000s as we will discuss later on.

During a period when investments in IT were tantamount to investments in computerization, the reported benefits were substantial. If the organization comes from a situation where they are used to handling e.g. the process of payroll manually, computerization offers massive opportunities for rationalization. Consequently, early investments in IT were, albeit costly, associated with direct effects in terms of efficiency through e.g. lay-offs. At the same time, the investments offered a substantial reduction in lead times, aiding the organization with benefits in terms of effectiveness. From this perspective, it is easy to see how earlier investments in IT (the first and second wave of IT, as seen below) were regarded as necessary and justifiable.

In general, investments in IT were handled in line with how other capital investments were handled. This infers that from an accounting perspective, organizations were keen on establishing the payback period in which the investment would become profitable. Hence, IT was seen as something that the organization utilized its capital on in order to achieve benefits in the future.

In the 1980s, Harvard sociologist Shoshana Zuboff (1988) described how computerization changed the very nature of work and power in three waves. The first of these waves is referred to as "Automate", where previously menial labor is automated through the use of IT with efficiency gains as a direct result. The second wave is referred to as "Informate", where what is currently happening in the organization becomes visible through informational representations, leading to increased quality in decision making. The third and final wave is referred to as "Transformate", where the consequences of digitalization reverberate through a rephrasing of the business model of the organization. Prof. Zuboff's work has had a substantial impact on the discourse of IT, resulting in numerous spinoffs and adaptations of the basic

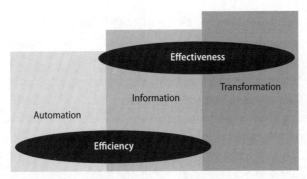

Figure 2.11 The balance between focus on efficiency and effectiveness in the three waves of IT.

model, such as Gartner's Pace Layered Approach with the corresponding Systems of Record, Differentiation and Innovation.

In Figure 2.11, we see the three waves of IT as identified by Zuboff (1988) portrayed in both time and impact on the organization, as well as the primary modus of justifying the investments. Initiatives such as the implementation of an enterprise system are regarded as primarily focusing on the Automate and Informate waves of IT, whereby the main focus in the evaluations was directed towards increased efficiency of operations. As previously noted in conjunction with the arguments put forth by Davenport (1998) on the issue of strategic competitive abilities, this is seen to transgress to the third wave of IT. Here, IT is regarded as a means through which an organization can reconfigure its very business.

Hence, as IT initiatives become more and more directed towards Transformate, through projects with impacts on not only the operative aspects, we expect to see a call for an increased focus on effectiveness as a means of evaluating the investments. This line of argumentation can be found in studies such as that by Xue, Ray and Sambamurthy (2012), where the generic strategy of the firm is linked to the IT portfolio (i.e. the total amount of IT projects currently active within the organization). Through their study using panel data, focusing on firms with either a cost leadership or differentiation strategy, they were able to identify differences in how IT should be evaluated. Figure 2.12 illustrates this related back to the distribution on a focus on efficiency versus effectiveness, or in Xue, Ray and Sambamurthy's vernacular, operational efficiency versus organizational innovation.

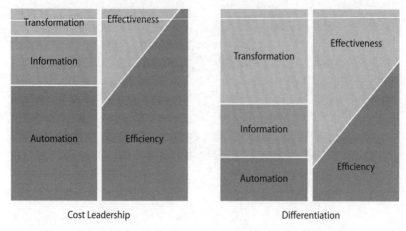

Figure 2.12 Cost Leadership versus Differentiation and the distribution of focus.

By the early 2000s, the overall perception of IT experienced a crisis. As previously noted, the Y2K scare along with the massive investments in ERP systems had left many organizations with a feeling of aversion directed towards IT. IT had, to put it bluntly, failed to live up to the almost savior-like expectations related to efficiency returns, something that the debate concerning what is referred to as the "Productivity Paradox" had already previously addressed.

The Productivity Paradox was first coined by Prof. Eric Brynjolfsson (1993) and can be summarized as the observation that computerization is basically seen everywhere except in the productivity statistics. Despite substantial investments, we had yet to see a corresponding spike in productivity on a macro economic level. This not seldom very heated debate reached its pinnacle in 2003 when Prof. Nicholas Carr published an article in the Harvard Business Review entitled "IT Doesn't Matter".

In this article, Carr compares IT with other previously widely diffused technologies such as railways, utility grids and telephones. The point of this comparison is that IT has ceased to offer a competitive advantage, and is now turning into an infrastructural resource. Previously, situating your plant in the vicinity of cheap electricity or cheap logistics offered you a competitive advantage, but with the technology becoming standard and commoditized, this advantage would turn out to be but temporary.

2 ENTER THE ACTORS

The consequence of this argumentation was senior managers not having to bother with understanding IT in the same manner as they did not need intricate understanding of how electricity is produced and distributed. Instead of being on the "bleeding edge" of technological development, businesses should focus on following the general use, adopting new technologies only after they had proved themselves valuable to the firms first to jump on the bandwagon.

Today, we see that this argumentation might have been oversimplified and the underlying assumption that IT was now (2003) moving into a stable state on account of it being fully developed could be considered lacking at best. At the same time, Carr's stance allowed managers to simplify the management agenda, and move towards regarding IT as a cost more than a potential source of innovation. The consequence of this thought is that of IT outsourcing, a phenomenon that saw an increase in popularity during the early 2000s.

Carr (2003) was later intermittently rebuffed and supported by the academic community, with McAffee and Brynjolfsson (2008) as one example where they showed that albeit being infrastructural in some aspects, it is also strategic and directly leads to competitive advantages for firms in IT-intensive environments. On one level, the entire debate concerning the value (or lack of value) of IT can be considered as caught in a stalemate where the very phenomenon in question avoids capture. IT in the form of servers, RFID tags or network switches has very little in common with a Facebook page for your community of customers, to name but one example.

THE INVESTMENT CONTEXT AND IT GOVERNANCE

IT Governance arose as an explicit topic during the late 1980s. With organizations becoming more and more dependent upon IT through computerization, along with the size of investments becoming more and more substantial, the necessity to set up a governance of the resource became pertinent. Governance in this respect refers to the establishment of settings for management, i.e. not the actual management itself but its prerequisites in the form of structures, processes and relational mechanisms (De Haes and Van Grembergen, 2005).

The issue of governance could be seen as stemming from work on agency theory and the principal-agent dilemma as developed by Jensen and Meckling

© STUDENTLITTERATUR 81

(1976). Here, the separation of ownership and control as seen in firms where the owners (principals) are not simultaneously operative managers (agents) calls for control mechanisms to ensure that the agents are actually working in the best interests of the principals. Hence, governance exists to alleviate the drawbacks of this separation in the form of information asymmetries, opportunistic behavior and moral hazards.

Within the academic field, the genealogy of IT Governance stems from work on Strategic Information Systems Planning (SISP), Information Resource Management (IRM) and IS Management (ISM). Earlier work was primarily focused on ensuring the internal operational efficiency of the IT function, yet this was later expanded towards looking into issues related to the alignment between IT and business. In this line of research (Sledgianowski, Luftman and Riley, 2006), the objective is to ensure, on a strategic as well as operative level, that IT isn't counteracting the overall intent of business, and that each initiative from IT is in line and contributes to the business. This relates the issue of strategic alignment to the economic concept of effectiveness rather than efficiency.

In 2004, MIT researchers Peter Weill and Jeanne W. Ross published a highly influential book on IT Governance, in one respect breaking through the glass ceiling that previously separated IT from business. In their research they had found that organizations with excellent IT Governance outperformed organizations with sub-par IT Governance. Hence, the link between IT Governance and overall performance of the organization was established in the mainstream, and there was an immediate response from industry and academia alike.

Weill and Ross (2004) describe IT Governance as the activity of specifying the decision rights and accountability framework to encourage desirable behavior in the use of IT. The novelty of this definition lies in the link between IT Governance and the factual beneficial use of IT. Hence, corporate IT was (conceptually) propelled away from the role of technology *ex-situ* to technology *in-situ*. IT was (in conflict with the previous ideas put forth by Carr (2003)) not something that corporate management could retreat from, but instead something that they had to control and be actively involved in.

The consequences of this raised popularity of IT Governance was twofold. On the one hand we saw an increase in the status assigned to IT Managers and people involved in the governance of IT. On the other hand, we saw a

Exhibit: IT Governance according to W&R

		Decision Domain									
		IT Principles		IT Architecture		IT Infrastructure Strategies		Business Applications Needs		IT Investment	
		Input	Decision	Input	Decision	Input	Decision	Input	Decision	Input	Decision
Governance Archetype	Business Monarchy										■
	IT Monarchy				■		■				
	Federal	■		■				■			
	IT Duopoly						■			■	
	Feudal										
	Anarchy										

■ Typical firm

Figure 2.13 IT Governance according to Weill and Ross (2004).

As previously noted, Weill and Ross' work on IT Governance immediately became the textbook for how organizations should think about their distribution of decision rights in terms of IT Governance. Figure 2.13 portrays the framework, with a division into decision domains and governance architectures. As shown, there is a division between who supplies the input for and who actually makes the decision related to each decision domain. The decision domains are divided into IT principles, IT architecture, IT infrastructure strategies, business application needs and IT investments. In terms of governance architecture, this categorization is based on loci of control, and a clear differentiation between IT and business.

radical increase in the level of formalization that IT underwent. Coupled with development related to what could be referred to as the "Supply and Demand Model" of IT, the distance between IT and business started to increase. This may seem as somewhat counter-intuitive given the aspiration of IT Governance towards making IT part of the corporate agenda, but it came as a direct consequence of the increased level of formalization (see Figure 2.14).

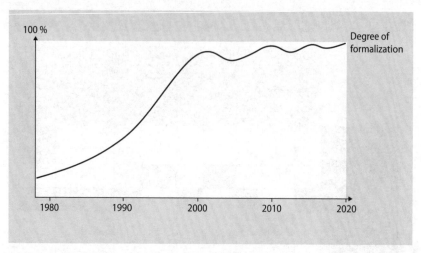

Figure 2.14 The shifting degree of formalization across time.

As seen in Figure 2.14, the degree of formalization has increased dramatically from the 1980s to the present state. The reasons for this can be attributed to both a legitimate need to have IT under control and to avoid risks associated with IT failures. As seen in the exhibit above, failures in large projects (such as enterprise systems) have been reported to have a substantial negative impact on the shareholder value of the firm. At the same time, the increased formalization of IT Governance also has a darker side, and we will spend some time in addressing this, albeit in a somewhat conjectural form.

One of the core ideas behind governance is, as previously noted, the aspiration of principals to ensure power over the agents. Hence, agents are not really free to act as they feel, but restricted in their actions through the very settings for action. This is poignantly illustrated by Brown (1978, p. 376):

> "Making decisions" is not the most important exercise of organizational power. Instead, this power is most strategically deployed in the design and imposition of paradigmatic frameworks within which the very meaning of such actions as "making decisions" is defined.

Governance in its ideal state is hence motivated, formulated and imposed by the principals in order to control the agents. In the form of IT, the principals have long had a tradition of retreat, whereas we need to ask ourselves the question of who has been the main driver behind the type of IT Governance that we see today. Who has been the principal in specifying IT Governance? This calls for a short description of one of the stronger players within corporate IT, namely the Chief Information Officer (CIO).

According to Grover et al. (1993, p. 108) the CIO is the "highest ranking IS executive who typically exhibits managerial roles requiring effective communication with top management, a broad corporate perspective in managing information resources, influence on organizational strategy, and responsibility for the planning of IT to cope with a firm's competitive

Exhibit: The four heads of the CIO Janus

In Magnusson (2010) and Magnusson & Bygstad (2013), a study of large, Swedish organizations and their IT Governance was conducted in collaboration with a major technology consulting firm. After interviews with 18 CIOs, the material was analyzed using theories from both Science and Technology Studies and the Sociology of Occupation and Work. From the results, two issues stand out. First, that there is a shift among CIOs from Professional to Corporate and further on to Marginal men. The Professional man has her main identity in the horizontal management of the IT function, and the professional values of the IT occupation. The Corporate man has her main identity in the vertical management, with a strong focus on the upper echelons of management. In terms of the Marginal man, which at present was the most prominent, she is torn between the two social worlds of the IT function and top management. Destined to never belong in either, she spends his time in between, resulting in the risk of a schizoid state.

An alternative description to this dismal view of the CIO is that of the four heads of Janus. According to legend, Janus was the Roman deity of transition, bridges and doors. Although usually depicted as a man with two heads, one facing backwards (to the past) and one forward (to the future), there stood a statue in the center of Rome with four heads. Janus simultaneously faced four forums, i.e. authorities in ancient Rome. As for the CIO, she is also poised between (at least) four authorities. There is the horizontal axis of projects versus maintenance (or the Roman reference of Transitorium and Pacis). In parallel with this, there is also the vertical axis of CEO versus top management (Julium and Romanum).

environment". Given this, we see that the role is positioned in the very intersection between business and IT, and that the CIO should act not only vertically but also horizontally. She is both the head of the IT function, and in many cases also part of senior management.

Early developments of this role in combination of the high risk characteristics of IT investments and initiatives lead to a situation where CIO tenure was bleak at best. Benjamin et al. (1984) went so far as to rephrase the acronym into "Career Is Over", since the CIO would exit the organization as soon as a major mistake was made (i.e. a project failed to deliver on time/budget/scope).

In response to this clear and present danger, the CIO needed two things: a clearer separation of accountability and an increased status within the organization. In terms of the first issue, this was to be achieved through first an increased formalization of what the IT function was actually responsible for delivering, resulting in an aspiration towards what we previously referred to as the "Supply and Demand model" of IT delivery. Here, the interface between the business and the IT function was formalized into the Demand being responsible for communicating the Business' requirements in an orderly fashion to the IT function. These demands could then be handled by forums where the demands were evaluated on the business case in question, i.e. what the expected cost and benefit would be. The business would be responsible for prioritizing what the IT function should devote its resources to. At the same time, the accountability related to actually realizing the benefits of the initiatives was equally pushed to the business. This left IT in a position where they would halt previous proactive initiatives, instead of focusing on supplying the organization with what was asked of them in a reactive manner.

At the same time, senior management was becoming more and more aware of the importance of IT for the strategic positioning of the firm. With IT being a resource that the organization's most critical processes were directly dependent upon and with IT being transformative in nature, there was an increased pull towards encompassing the CIO into the Board of Directors. Since IT Governance clearly was something that could add to superior results (in line with the reasoning by Weill and Ross, 2004), many organizations saw this as something natural.

The result of these developments was a situation where the formalization of IT Governance quickly became in vogue. In terms of best practice, IT

Exhibit: The contingencies of the CIO reporting structures

In the quest for strategic influence and status, there has long been a prevailing notion that the optimal reporting structure for the CIO would be to the CEO or equivalent. This is based on the general misconception that IT has always (as opposed to previously never) strategic impacts on the organization, inherited from the previous discussion on the value and role of IT.

Banker et al. (2011) nuanced this perception in a quantitative study where the strategic positioning of firms, their financial performance and the CIO reporting structure was investigated. Strategic positioning was done following Michael Porter's generic strategies of Cost Leadership versus Differentiation. As the results showed, in terms of performance, there is no one-size-fits-all optimal reporting structure. In firms categorized as following the Cost Leadership strategy, the optimal reporting structure was from CIO to Chief Financial Officer (CFO). In terms of firms categorized as following the Differentiation strategy, the optimal reporting structure was directly to the CEO.

The rationale behind this is that depending on strategic positioning, the firm's focus on different aspects of IT. As for the Cost Leadership firm, keeping tabs on the IT spending is of the utmost importance, and the competitive advantage is not related to early adoption of state-of-the-art IT but primarily to cost control. This warrants a perception of IT as simply a cost of operations, and hence the CIO should report to the CFO. As for the Differentiation firms, IT may very well prove to be a prerequisite for differentiation, and hence the strategic dialogue between the CIO and CEO becomes warranted.

A possible criticism of the study lies in the problems with categorizing a firm as either/or in accordance with the generic strategies. A firm should perhaps be perceived as employing a heterogeneous bundle of strategies, making it practically impossible to treat the role of IT as one thing. In a time where firms are increasingly becoming dependent upon technology and where competition comes not only from previous competitors but also from new entrants, this may be an altogether different situation. In the case of car manufacturing, for instance, Google has not previously been considered a competitor but may very well be so in the future with its current investments in driverless vehicles. In the case of hotels, new actors such as Airbnb.com is mediating the sub-let of apartments, castles, boats and houses, turning the individual homeowner into a competitor.

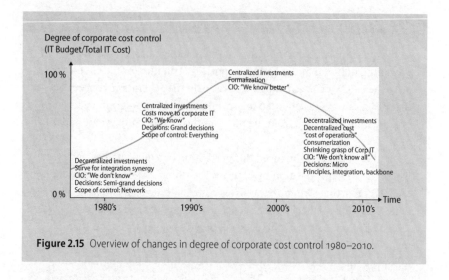

Figure 2.15 Overview of changes in degree of corporate cost control 1980–2010.

Governance was: formulated by the CIO (or the IT Steering Committee), involved a highly formalized demand and supply model, a decentralization of benefits realization and the CIO reporting directly to the CEO of the organization. We will discuss the results of this below, as they are currently unfolding.

In conjunction with the increased formalization of IT Governance, there has long been a corresponding development of corporate cost control over IT spending. During the 1980s, most investments in IT were decentralized, with department managers et cetera commissioning the design and development of customized solutions fitting their particular needs. In this state of affairs, decisions were relatively small and the scope of control for the CIO was mainly directed towards ensuring or supporting integration and development.

During the 1990s, with the increased scope of functionality of enterprise systems and the increase in size of each investment, it became natural to halt these decentralized investments and aspire global synergies through enterprise-wide solutions, reaching its pivotal moment in the early 2000s with the last wave of major ERP investments. At this time, the corporate cost control did not leave any room for additional investments, since everything had to be focused on ensuring the success of the major investments. This could be perceived as the golden age for the CIOs, with their scope of control being almost complete, and their role as internal suppliers being principally unchallenged.

Exhibit: To centralize or decentralize IT

In a study conducted in 2010 (Magnusson, 2013), we present the case of a large public university and their organization of the IT function. Relating the issue of whether IT should be decentralized or centralized back to both the concentration theory (that IT brings with it massive economies of scale for its internal organization) and the consonance theory (that organization should mirror or be aligned with governance, as proposed by Joan Woodward), we show how the organization of IT displays tendencies of "instinctive centralization".

In the case, the university was seen as having followed the general trends of organizing the IT function during the past 15 years, from centralization, towards decentralization in the 1990s and towards a recentralization in the early noughties. The recent initiative was one of centralization, where the IT department itself was pushing the agenda through the rationale of cost-efficiency and economies of scale. The highly decentralized organization (the rest of the university) was adamant towards having their currently decentralized IT resources expropriated.

Despite not being inclined towards centralizing IT, they understood the rationale behind coordination benefits associated with IT, and initiated a call for "Local Shared Services", where they would pool IT resources between geographically adjacent organizational entities. With the original centralization initiative having failed, this was regarded as a small comfort for the central IT department and a sign that decentralization had won.

After a couple of years, the Local Shared Services arrived at a position where they saw a necessity for aspiring to an increased coordination between the said shared services. Hence, they initiated a new form of organization, i.e. a "Cross Shared Service" organization, where they appointed resources and responsibilities to a separate organizational entity commissioned to make sure that economies of scale were secured and cost-efficiency achieved. Through this, the resistance to centralization resulted in a situation with more centralization than was originally intended. Utilizing the theory of Social Transformation Processes (Strandgaard Pedersen and Dobbin, 2006), this was analyzed as imitation, transmutation and hybridization, with the conclusion that the organization of IT seems to be endowed with what we refer to as instinctive centralization. In other words, IT at this particular university displayed parallel logics of centralization and decentralization. This paradoxical state is seen as more than simply what Albert and Whetten

(1985) would refer to as "Ideographic" organization, i.e. an organization having dual identities. Instead, we see the organization of technology as institutionally entwined with the changing content of technology, and that we will continue to see instinctive centralization in parallel with decentralization.

In the wake of these investments, formalization reached its pivotal moment. At the same time, consumer oriented IT started to have a major impact on the lives of people, giving them an alternative perspective on IT as not something cumbersome and complex, but rather as something more or less intuitive. By the late first decade of the 21st century, internet-based technologies had reached such a state that new solutions built directly on this platform were quickly becoming a viable alternative even for organizations. New delivery models such as Software as a Service (SaaS) and Cloud Computing were becoming mainstream, reducing the thresholds and making it possible to try new solutions for free before making the decision of investing in them.

Hence, the users of this period were the first to be in a situation where they could select, without massive initial costs, their own solution for business analysis (to name but one example), implement the solution locally and simply rent it for a nominal fee if they found it to their liking. The result of this (in conjunction with the market identifying this possibility and building their business model for this particular purpose) was twofold.

First, IT changed from being something that was primarily centrally controlled to something that was controlled in a hybrid model. Organizations still boasted central solutions for functions such as CRM and BI, yet at the same time they saw an increase in the disparate use of alternative solutions (see Exhibit). Second, IT started to change from primarily being something that was invested in (with a focus on Capital Expenditure, CAPEX), to something that was simply perceived as the cost of operations (with a focus on Operational Expenditure, OPEX). According to the industry analysts at Gartner, the level of corporate cost control for IT in 2019 will have declined to 10 percent. IDC puts the figure at 20 percent by 2018. The level of IT costs that are not under central control are often referred to as "Shadow IT", or maverick IT spending.

Combining these two developments of increased formalization with

Exhibit: The Case of the wandering CRM system

A Swedish firm comprised of sixty-odd(-eight?) subsidiaries globally dispersed commenced an internal IT audit in order to find possibilities of cost reduction and efficiency gains. In line with this, the CIO identified a strange pattern of use for the global CRM solution. As it turned out, some of the firms within the group were not using the CRM solution, which raised some concerns. The following conversation transpired between the CIO and the local CEO.

CIO: I see that you are not using the group's CRM system?

Local CEO: No, we did not find it suitable to our needs in relation to distributed sales teams. We decided to use [a global SaaS based CRM vendor] instead.

CIO: Alright, that's fine. How is it working for you?

Local CEO: Well… it was working great…

CIO: Yeah, what happened?

Local CEO: Well, the former Sales Director made the decision and got it up and running. For about a year it worked perfectly, but last month he left the organization to join a competing firm.

CIO: So?

Local CEO: Well… Since then we have tried to get access to the information in terms of customers, meetings et cetera, but as it turns out we don't have access to it. To avoid going through the corporate hoops in getting the investment, the Sales Director simply purchased the licenses with his own credit card and took it as an expense. Now, when we talk to the vendor they say that there is nothing they can do about it.

CIO: What? You gotta be kiddin' me? So, all your customer data is now in the hands of our competitors? How are you going to solve this?

Local CEO: Well… We have signed a new agreement with the vendor and have started up again. So, things are pretty much back to normal. We have lost a sizeable part of our market share though, but I am sure we will be able to turn this around eventually.

As it turned out, taking the issue to court to get access to the customer data proved too hard on account of the data not being in one particular place (or rather the servers). Albeit a sign of cloud solutions still being in their infancy, protracted legal procedures and contracts pose a substantial threat to organizations that fall wanting in terms of control of Shadow IT.

decreased corporate cost control (see Figure 2.16), we find IT Governance experiencing somewhat of a crisis. The models used for governing IT are dependent upon the factual level of control that the models infer, and if there is a gap between the perceived and factual level of control, IT Governance needs to change. The alternative to this is imposed control, and as we have seen so far this does little but further alienate the users.

So, this rather bleak and dismal perception of the current state of IT Governance may leave the reader in a state of bewilderment. To counteract this, we will approach the issue from a different perspective.

In line with the reasoning by Carr (2003), we could see the turn from CAPEX to OPEX, from corporate cost control to shadow IT as signs of the technology itself actually reaching a more stable state through becoming pervasive. This interpretation would go hand in hand with developments regarding what is referred to as Bring Your Own Device (BYOD) and the Internet of Everything. In terms of BYOD, this development calls for the necessity of accepting personal devices from your users into the IT environment of your particular organization. Hence, the IT infrastructure needs to be able to accommodate a vast array of different devices, with disparate protocols, levels of security et cetera. Previous notions of control

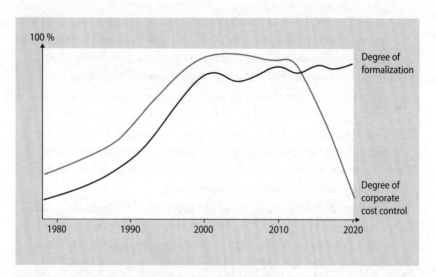

Figure 2.16 Comparison of degree of control and formalization.

in terms of the infrastructure are hence toppled by the wishes and desires of people to bring their own devices to work.

This development signals two things. First, that technology is personal, and that individuals with a particular preference should not be forced into device-level conformity just because they are entering their work environment. Second, and perhaps also foremost, it signals that the divide between the personal and professional spheres is starting to be blurred. Today, the average user in Western organizations is *IT native*, born into the technology rather than migrated into it. Hence, their personal use of technology is equally (or in many cases) more complex than their professional use, leading to entirely different perspectives on what technology is and what its role is. With IT becoming pervasive and work following us around all the time through a constant access to emails, instant messages and BI, the average user of today is in an entirely different position in terms of knowledge and experience with regard to IT.

> The most profound technologies are those that disappear. They weave themselves into the fabric of everyday life until they are indistinguishable from it.
>
> DR, MARK WEISER, FORMER CTO, XEROX PARK

Can this then perhaps be seen in line with Carr (2003) and his notions that IT is becoming an infrastructural technology like utility grids or railways? That despite not being an electrical engineer, the services of the utility firms are packaged to such an extent that I can choose vendors? The comparability of services and the interoperability through common standards and interfaces has led to a situation where we might at least to some extent acknowledge Carr's line of reasoning.

Relating this line of argument to the issue of platforms in general and Enterprise System Platforms in particular, we find a situation where the blueprint for a new distribution of authority and accountability is displayed in the very notion of the platform. The choice of platform provider is far from arbitrary, and requires substantial knowledge and experience. As for the choice of apps or added functionality offered on the platform, this is an entirely different matter. With (close to) automatic integration of apps into the platform, we could conceive a situation where the savvy technology user could

Exhibit: Technology debt in the study of investment options

Every decision involves the dismissal of other options. In the case of IT investments, this axiom holds particularly true. Making a decision in relation to IT involves choosing a path and inviting lock-in effects, switching costs and opportunity costs. Hence, IT investments simultaneously limit and support future options. In Magnusson and Bygstad (2014) we propose a theory for better understanding this decision maker's dilemma in relation to IT investments.

The theory proposes that technology debt is owed by the past and present decision makers (CIOs) to the future decision makers, and that decisions are limited by three factors. First, there is the institutional environment consisting of the perceptions of IT residing within the organization. Second, there is the institutional logic, or the strategic intent in relation to IT within the organization. Third, there is the installed base, i.e. the current situation in terms of systems et cetera.

Technology debt is regarded as the cost associated with limitations in maneuverability in future options, and each decision can either increase (lend) or decrease (amortize) the debt, i.e. increase or decrease the maneuverability.

The theory proposes both a process and typological model to study and measure technology debt, and was initially tested on the case of a large, public university in 2013. As the findings showed, the past ten years of large, IT related investments had followed a specific pattern where the technology debt associated with the IT staff had increased with each investment. At the same time, there had been an amortization of technology debt in terms of the users. In other words, the organization had consequentially borrowed from their own staff in order to please the users, with an increase in sick-leaves, staff turnover et cetera as a direct result.

The theory is proposed to be used for both assessing the potential impacts on maneuverability of present investments (to be included in the business case methodology), and, to be used as a means for IT auditors in their concurrent auditing. Four more cases have been conducted and are currently awaiting publication.

make his or her own decision on purchasing an app within what is referred to as an Enterprise App Store (EAS). This app could be in the form of one out of many CRM solutions provided for the platform, and its deployment would

2 ENTER THE ACTORS

be immediate. Hence, we see a situation where the platform as such opens up for harboring not only the demand driven innovation of the previous IT Governance settings, but also the user-driven innovation that is now handled through Shadow IT. We will return to this issue in more detail later on in this book.

Implementation

For many organizations, enterprise system projects constitute the largest, riskiest and most important projects that they will ever be involved in, and hence there has been a substantial amount of research into the phenomenon.

In terms of the implementation of enterprise systems, there have been multiple reports of the majority of projects failing. According to industry analyst data cited by Klingberg and Magnusson (2011), 80 percent of all enterprise systems implementations fail to deliver on time, budget and scope. With regard to how many of the projects are actually considered failures by the implementing organization, this is much less, closer to 40 percent. In terms of failed projects, the issue at hand is a complex one. First, we see that the measurement of success in terms of projects is primarily an issue of internal project efficiency and ability to deliver according to schedule. Hence, the project's ability to deliver on time, budget and scope will be primarily dependent upon the feasibility of the project charter, i.e. the business case that led to the investment and initiation of the project. In cases where costs are hard to assess and forecast, such as in massive, cross-functional IT projects, all three variables defining the project will be guesswork at best. Added to this, the dependence upon internal and external suppliers of support (such as internal support and external consultants), the issue of communication also comes into play. Is the organization ready to communicate its needs? Do they understand the massive implications of the project? Do they understand the internal dependencies between functionality and processes? In many of the cases that we have seen, the answer to these questions is undoubtedly no. If the organization has a hard time specifying what it needs, what is the probability of the implemented enterprise system actually supporting this?

From this perspective, it is not surprising that enterprise system implementations have a high reported probability of failure. In addition to this, there is also the political issue of short-stocking the expected costs and up-playing the expected benefits, in order to get this particular project prioritized in the internal prioritization process. With a strong sense of need comes the issue that you will do your utmost to get your investment accepted. With organizations today having ample prior experience from enterprise system implementations, and projects still failing, this could be the most important of the identified reasons for project failure. This is, however, related to how organizations conduct their post-implementation reviews of their investments, an issue we will return to later on in this chapter.

There is a challenge when discussing the implementation of such a diverse phenomenon as enterprise systems, with it spanning the full scope between on-site, traditional monolith ERP solutions to a Software as a Service (SaaS) and Platform as a Service (PaaS) and incremental add-ons. In addition to this, we will approach implementation from a lifecycle perspective, dividing it into three phases. First, we will address the issues related to pre-implementation, followed by the actual implementation and then the post-implementation. In practice, these phases are not as easily separated as we will present them here.

To make the process of implementation more accessible, we will focus on the case of Hestra as depicted in Magnusson, Klingberg, Enquist, Oskarsson & Gidlund (2010). The reason for this single case approach is that we feel that this case highlights many of the aspects that an organization needs to address before, during and after the implementation. Hestra (Hestra Inredningar AB) is a family-owned medium-sized firm located in the center of Sweden. For the past 100 years, Hestra has focused on shop fitting, making them one of the oldest and largest actors in the market. They have operations in several countries in the Nordic region, and are financially sound.

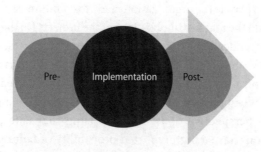

Figure 2.17 The three phases of implementation.

PRE-IMPLEMENTATION

Before there is action, we assume that there is intent. In terms of enterprise systems, this intent ranges across a multitude of different rationales. In some cases, the motive for investing or re-investing in an enterprise system is related to political issues, such as in the case of Coop, a Nordic retailing chain with subsidiaries in the Nordic countries. Here, the battle for what enterprise system the organization should select became a battle between local CEOs for setting the agenda in not having to change their current system, as the organization as a whole was to consolidate from three enterprise systems to one. In other cases, it could be an issue of necessity, such as in the Swedish ball bearing company SKF's implementation of SAP as a means for replacing obsolete information systems. It could also, such as in the case of Harley Davidson's much-cited implementation of a Supplier Relationship Management solution be the execution of a new strategy, where the enterprise system becomes a necessary prerequisite. In other cases, it is a matter of "dressing the bride" for future owners, choosing the same solution as the intended or expected acquiring firm to improve the value of the firm.

Regardless of motives, the process of implementing a (new) enterprise system starts with a feeling of need, want or desire. When organizations start to identify and formulate this need into a requirement, they have entered into the pre-implementation phase.

At Hestra the initiation of intent came with the old enterprise system not having been upgraded for several years. This resulted in the necessity for either upgrading the existing system or replacing it with a newer one. Hence, the motive for the initiative came from bare necessities, with the current system not offering the necessary support for operations.

As a first step, the CEO of Hestra hired a new CFO. With the CFO often being the instigator of an enterprise systems investment (primarily through increased control over costs through the new system), they chose a CFO with previous experience from procuring an enterprise system for a neighboring firm. The CFO in question was intent on simply upgrading the existing system in place. The functional fit between what Hestra wanted to do and what the upgrade of the existing system would result in was considered to be sufficient, and the CFO quickly set about creating a business case for the planned investment.

On presenting the business case to the CEO, the CFO was, however, highly surprised to see that what he had thought was the objective was really pretty far from target. Instead of simply wanting to upgrade the existing system, the CEO was searching for ways in which Hestra as a company could be improved. This caught the CFO quite off guard, but in interviews that we held with him a year after the meeting, he was very pleased to see that the CEO widened the scope of the assignment.

This highlights one of the many pitfalls of upgrading or investing in an enterprise system, i.e. the question of scope. In assuming that the main objective was to upgrade an existing system, the CFO was acting well in line with what could be expected of him. He saw the immediate need of expanding the functionality of the existing system, and chose his approach based on this. Instead of looking at the business directly, identifying issues that could be addressed through a new enterprise system and through this aspiring business related benefits rather than expanded functions.

So, rather taken aback, the CFO returned to his office and started to think about how he could move ahead with the assignment of improving Hestra.

After the assignment had been given to the CFO, he immediately set about discussing ways in which the intended improvements to business could be identified and communicated as part of the enterprise systems procurement process. The outset of this has traditionally been identifying key areas of functionality, and specifying these in a detailed manner. For instance, the buying enterprise could specify a demand as "Does the system support alphanumerical descriptions of items with at least 30 characters?", or "Does the system support the adding of new customers into the database?" As seen, for the purpose of buying something that is highly standardized, most vendors of enterprise systems would probably answer the majority of questions in the affirmative, hence making the material in the form of a functional specification relatively lacking in value as a basis for selecting the most appropriate solution.

Instead of following this traditional approach, the CFO initiated a series of workshops with co-workers assigned to roles of sub-process owners in the organization. These individuals were the informal leaders of the organization, the people with the highest competency and experience in terms of their respective sub-processes. These individuals were asked to participate in two separate workshops.

The first workshop focused on identifying the full process of Hestra,

Exhibit: Potential effects of ERP implementations

In a study of Finnish companies published in 2007, researcher Oana Velcu identified differences in benefits stemming from whether the implementation was business- or technology led, as she refers to it. In terms of technology led, the outset of the implementation and its subsequent management is from the technology side of the organization. In other words, the main objective is identified as changing the ERP system itself, expanding or replacing functionality. This is the primary objective of the project, and the subsequent impact on business is secondary at best. At the other range of this spectrum, business-led implementations are instigated and managed from a business perspective, immediately focusing on the expected benefits in terms of more efficient processes and more effective business.

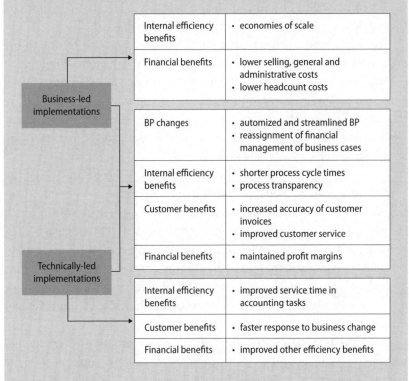

Figure 2.18 Differences in benefits from business- vs technically led implementations.

from a sales order coming in, to the customer invoice being paid. During a full day, the participants of the workshop focused on describing (using a wall and several stacks of post-it notes) their individual sub-processes, and how these were handed off with the neighboring sub-processes. During this session, the participants worked towards getting an understanding of the overall process, and what happened up- and downstream from their own area of expertise.

The results of this workshop was both a new understanding of the complete process with all its hand-offs between different departments, as well as a formalized description of how the organization currently operated, i.e. an "as-is" process model. The consequences of the increased understanding of what happened at the hand-offs resulted in ideas in terms of changes to the system, as well as an ability of the participants to identify ways in which they could prevent mistakes and problems further down the line.

For the second workshop, the participants were asked to design the process in a manner that they saw as optimal. This was something that at the time was considered to be little more than a thought-experiment by the participants. They had a hard time understanding why they should specify this, since they saw little chance of it resulting in any change in the processes. Nevertheless, they set about in the same manner as during the first workshop with a white wall and a deck of post-it notes.

In specifying the process as it should be (the "to-be" process), the participants utilized their previously identified problems in hand-offs as well as the sub-process internal inefficiencies. They specified ways in which the process could be made more efficient through automating parts of it, reducing sources of manual error and sub-optimization through "tricky" shortcuts previously employed with resulting downstream problems. They created a process model for how the process should be, and at the end of the day they were highly animated in terms of how much of an improvement this could really be.

After the two workshops, the CFO was in a situation where he had managed to secure several necessary components for the upcoming enterprise system procurement and subsequent implementation. First, he had secured an understanding of how the current process (as-is) was configured at Hestra. Second, he had interesting ideas in terms of how the future process could be designed (to-be) in order for Hestra to be more efficient in its operations.

Exhibit: Hakim and Hakim's (2010) prerequisites for ERP acceptance

In a study of ERP implementations in Iran, Hakim and Hakim (2010) presented a four-phased model for establishing the necessary prerequisites for ERP acceptance. The model along with a simplification is presented in Table 2.2.

Table 2.2 Adopted and expanded from Hakim and Hakim (2010).

Phase	Question	Simplification	Level
1	Has the ERP implementation been introduced as part of a corporate strategic objective?	Is it legitimate?	Strategic
2	Is ERP beneficial for the organization?	Is it rational?	Tactical
3	Is the organization ready to adopt and adapt to ERP?	Is it possible?	Tactical
4	Which constraining factors and risks can be identified?	Is it feasible?	Operative

Third, he had managed to involve the informal leaders of the organization into the enterprise systems project.

For the next step, the process blueprints were used as a foundation for initiating a dialogue with potential vendors of enterprise systems fitting the bill. After an initial scanning of the market, three vendors were identified as plausible, and hence a dialogue was initiated with all three.

This dialogue involved communicating the scope of the intended system through a brief functional description and the two sets of blueprints. In these, Hestra had identified specifically important areas of improvement, which they expected the vendors to respond to in terms of how their specific solution would lead to the new process being operational. This process can be seen as the Request for Proposal (RFP) or Request for Information (RFI), with the intent of giving the prospective vendors the necessary information to respond with a feasible presentation of the solution. In other words, it is a first step towards establishing a dialogue between the vendors and the organization.

After initiating the dialogue with the three selected vendors, the CFO scheduled meetings during which the vendors would present their respective solutions to Hestra's request. This involved inviting the group of sub-process owners to represent Hestra, with these individuals being well in tune with the requested improvements in operations.

Each vendor was given half a day for presentations and discussion. During this time, they would have access to the facilities and the individuals involved in making the decision in terms of which vendor Hestra should choose. The first vendor (the vendor already present through the existing system), was asked to respond to how an upgrade and customization would look in operations. Unfortunately, this vendor failed to attend the scheduled meeting, and in terms of their formal response to the RFP they identified a shortage of consultants that would be able to assist the future implementation. In addition to this, their response included the highest estimate in price of the three prospective solutions.

The second vendor attended the presentation and was well received by the sub-process owners and the CFO. Their solution gave a good impression with the best functional fit, yet the presentation was completely devoid of references to Hestra's operations and the identified process improvements. Instead, the representative of the vendor showed the wide range of functionality that was available in the enterprise system. This was perceived as a weakness in terms of the prospective relationship, with the vendor not wanting to discuss Hestra's individual issues and potential improvements.

The third vendor took a different approach. With the RFP being highly detailed in terms of how the current process was configured and what process changes Hestra wanted to pursue, they spent an estimated 100 hours in preparing their presentation. They asked and were given access to the existing enterprise system and the underlying data, and performed a setup of their solution directly based on these data. They customized the solution to fit the identified needs of Hestra, and when it was time for a presentation they sat directly in the system working through the process and discussing additional avenues of improvements.

When reconvening after the three presentations (the first vendor was given a second chance which resulted in an acceptable impression), the overall impression was that the third vendor was the winning solution. Although not having support for two of the functional areas requested, they gave the impression of understanding Hestra's issues and this was prioritized higher than functional fit. After a Request For Tender (RFT) and a subsequent negotiation the deal was signed and Hestra could enter into a process of implementation.

So what can we learn from the way that Hestra handled their pre-implementation phase? Related back to the previous discussion on how the success of an investment in enterprise systems could be assessed we see that the process was relatively efficient with a minimum of meetings (two workshops) and a relatively swift process from initiation to negotiation. In terms of the issue of effectiveness, we can use Hakim and Hakim's (2010) model. In terms of the strategic level, the legitimacy of the investment was supported by this being initiated from the office of the CEO, with the CFO as project owner. It was presented as a means for improving operations at Hestra, and not simply as the upgrade of an existing system (which could be regarded as simply an act of necessity). As for the tactical level, the rationality of the investment was identified and made clear to the organization through the participation of the sub-process owners in the specification of the as-is and to-be process, and the gap analysis of the necessary improvements. In specifying this, and allowing the informal leaders of the organization to be involved, the rationality was made clear. The participation of the sub-process owners was also a means for securing the plausibility of the investment, with the improvements being instigated by the same people as would be involved in its execution and upcoming operations. As for the pitfalls on the tactical level, this would be handled in the implementation phase, which could be regarded as something that should have been part of a proof-of-concept process. Hence, this could have been included in the RFP, but was omitted due to a desire to push things forward as fast as possible.

IMPLEMENTATION

The implementation of an enterprise system is a high-risk, resource-intensive project with the purpose of putting the enterprise system into operation. The reason for this high level of risk and the required resources can be attributed to both a complex technical solution (with the enterprise system being placed into an existing information system environment with a high degree of interdependence with other systems) and a subsequent change in the processes of the firm (constituting the improvement to operations). In addition to these difficulties, we have to consider that the shift in enterprise system has to be done while the organization continues to function, i.e. without the processes stopping or the existing systems experiencing downtime. To use an analogy from sports, this could be compared to performing a heart transplant on a participator in the New York marathon, during the actual marathon. With a constant strain on the body, constant movement and the inability to slow down, pulling this off would be quite a feat.

At Hestra, the implementation was scheduled to be finalized before the end of the year, making the balancing of books as easy as possible. This ambition may seem intuitive, yet at the same time it is often counterproductive. For firms with a fiscal year equal to the calendar year, this results in the main push in the implementation being scheduled for the end of the year. For many firms this poses a problem, with increased order handling, scheduled vacations for co-workers and the holiday seasons coming up. Hence, this is the time of year when the corporate resources that could be utilized are at a minimum, and planning for a peak in workload may not be warranted by how much easier this makes things for the CFO.

Exhibit: The impact of project failures on stock prices

In a highly acclaimed article in the Strategic Information Systems Journal in 2009, Bharadwaj, Keil and Mähring presented the result of a cross-sectional study of the impacts of public announcement of IT project failures on the market value of firms. As the results show, the authors were able to identify a 2 percent mean cumulative abnormal drop ($490 million in the sample) in stock prices for a two-day event window. Hence, the direct effects of publicly announcing the failure of a large-scale IT project are directly detrimental to shareholder value. Not surprisingly, the drop was particularly severe for firms with a history of previous IT failures, and for projects involving a new system rather than operational problems of existing systems.

These findings result in an interesting set of questions that would be necessary for the listed firm involved in a large scale IT project. How do we handle a public announcement of project failure? Should this be something that we plan for in chartering the project? How do we handle the negative impacts of announcing the failure? The study sheds new light on the famous words of Benjamin Franklin: "If you fail to plan, you are planning to fail": Planning to fail may be a necessity, at least for listed firms.

The implementation started directly after Hestra and the vendor had signed the agreement. As a first step, the project was planned and resources were assigned. With the sub-process owners being highly involved in the pre-implementation, it was decided that these individuals should continue to play a vital role in the project.

One of the regular difficulties with an enterprise system implementation is that the project becomes dependent upon external resources and competency in the form of consultants. These professionals enter the organization with varying levels of knowledge in terms of what the business really is, but they

Exhibit: ERP Implementation as participatory design

Participatory design (PD) can be seen as a set of principles focusing on the emancipation of the worker into an active member of the development team. This approach was developed in Scandinavia during the 1970s and 80s, and had a strong link to Marxist ideologies and the ideas about the power attributed to being involved in the design of one's own work (Spinuzzi, 2005).

Suchman (1995:viii) defines PD as concerned with "a more human, creative and effective relationship between those involved in technology's design and its use". Following up on this, Kensing & Blomberg (1998) state that PD is concerned with three main issues: Politics of design, the Nature of participation and Methods and tools. Out of these three issues, this paper focuses on the Nature of participation, with a particular emphasis on the cooperation and knowledge integration between users and Innovators of technology.

A number of articles have addressed the issue of PD in relation to ERP implementations, such as the formerly mentioned Pries-Heje & Dittrich (2009), Wagner & Piccoli (2007), Taylor (1998) and Fischer et al. (2004). Central to the findings is that user involvement and the use of PD is a way of facilitating successful ERP implementation.

Vilpola (2008) takes a different approach towards the involvement of users in ERP implementation projects. She takes a User-Centered Design (UCD) approach by building a method on the 1999 ISO 13407 standard. In her own words (2008:2), this is an attempt that "... focuses on the requirements of both users and the organization ... improving the usability of the system by early user involvement and continuous iteration ..."

are generic experts within fields such as the typical enterprise system, project methodologies or change management. As a rule of thumb, we could regard the consulting part of the implementation as 75 percent of the total direct cost, with licenses and maintenance fees constituting the remaining 25 percent.

One of the main risks here is that the organization becomes too dependent upon the external consultants, and retreats from the project itself. This is a mistake in two ways. First, the project as it was agreed upon in the contracts usually involves participation from the organization's co-workers. The consultants need a receiving part, and somebody that could guide them in making sure that they do not implement functionality that is counter-productive to the specific situation. Regardless of how well the organization has prepared the requirements specification for the solution, there will be a need for a continuous dialogue between the consultants and the co-workers. The rule of thumb here is that for every hour that the consultants spend, the organization has to assign three hours. If the organization fails to make these resources available, the project will run the risk of deviating from the plan as well as delimiting the future success of the solution in terms of fit. Second, if the organization fails to assign the necessary resources, there will be no knowledge transfer from the consultants to the co-workers, and hence the organization will be stuck in a situation of future dependence. In other words, they run the risk of having to keep the consultants on site in the future, at high costs and high risk.

At Hestra, this situation was handled in an innovative manner. With the sub-process owners having been intimately involved in the selection of the solution, they decided to stay on in the project as "super-users". In addition to this, they decided that with them being informal leaders and well positioned in the organization, they were the perfect teachers for getting the rest of the staff involved in using the new system. Hence, they set about building educational material from the process maps that they had previously created, setting up routines directly related to how the processes should be executed in the system by the various users. This required them to get extensive training in the system, but it also facilitated a knowledge transfer from consultant to co-worker before the implementation was finalized.

After this, they were the ones responsible for conducting the on-site training of the future users, in a language that the users were well accustomed to and at a level of detail that was appropriate for the upcoming tasks. The

Exhibit: Critical success factors of enterprise system implementations.

Magnusson, Nilsson and Carlsson (2004a) proposed a consummate model for the factors influencing the probability of success in an enterprise system implementation. Developed as industry research for SAP during 2004, it summarized the previous findings from research into a model divided into four categories of critical success factors (CSFs).

Figure 2.19 ERP Scorecard (adopted from Magnusson, Nilsson and Carlsson, 2004a).

In terms of Management, the first factor is related to having an IT strategy that is aligned with the overarching business strategy. In the case of ERP investments, the rationale usually lies in striving for economies of scale through standardization, centralization and consolidation. If this is in contrast with your firm's strategy, such as for a firm with a decentralized organizational setup and a striving for agility rather than efficiency, this would be tantamount to a lack of alignment. The second factor is related to having a strong Leadership capable of handling the investment through its various phases, and Support is related to how Top Management signals support for the investment. Competence refers to the level of previous experience from cross-functional, large-scale projects for IT induced changes.

In terms of Project, the first factor is that of having fundamental experience of working in teams. Management refers to the organization having project management expertise, and Plan refers to the organization having clear processes, procedures and methodologies for project work. This includes project management methodologies and templates for project plans et cetera. External refers to the organization's ability to use external consultants while at the same time securing an active knowledge transfer to avoid future lock-ins and consultancy dependence.

In terms of Organization, the factors focus on having an aptitude for change, a culture that breeds knowledge sharing and cross-functional work, as well as having formalized understanding of the current setup of processes and strategies for internal communication.

In terms of System, the factors focus on both the technical aspects of the coming installation (having control over and understanding of your technological environment), and the role of the prospective users and their role in the adoption of the ERP system.

result of this was that the consultancy dependence was kept at a minimum, and that the future users controlled the adaptation during adoption.

Training the future users resulted in additional adaptations being brought into the system, and in the end the project reached a situation where the scheduled go-live (shifting from the old systems to the new, i.e. making all new transactions into the new system) was necessary to move ahead from the beginning of the fiscal year. As noted in the introduction to this section, this is often the case with firms at first trying to simplify the responsibilities of the CFO, but subsequently understanding that it may not be worth risking operations.

The strain on the organization during primarily the mid- to latter part of the implementation was substantial. To counteract this, Hestra had hired substitutes to fill in the regular positions of the sub-process owners, who at this time had to spend all of their time on the project. Despite this, the strain on the sub-process owners was massive, and there were accounts of faintings and breakdowns.

In the end, the system went live without any major hiccups, yet with the historic data being kept in the old enterprise system. Hence, the new enterprise system did not lead to the dismantling but rather moth-bagging of the old one.

POST-IMPLEMENTATION

After the new enterprise system went live, the consultants exited Hestra and operations went back to more or less normal. The sub-process owners returned to their old jobs and the substitutes were let go. When asked about the project in retrospect, they referred to it as a great learning experience, though highly strenuous and difficult. Previous research has identified a risk in making individuals involved in the implementation project return to their old jobs, since this would amount to a regression in their careers, yet this was not perceived as a problem at Hestra. This is discussed in more detail in Bala and Venkatesh (2013), on changes in job characteristics throughout the implementation process.

In terms of the so valuable process maps created in the two sets of workshops, these quickly became obsolete due to a strong focus on the routines and manuals for executing the process in the enterprise system. As researchers, we considered this to be a mistake, yet the organization does not show any signs at this time of lacking up-to-date process maps

Exhibit: The business of being a user

In Pollock and Hyysalo (2014), the role of the user in the diffusion of enterprise systems is investigated. The study finds that as vendors they try to attract emotional investments from the users and utilize the users as references for continued sales and marketing. Through introducing the notion of "reference actor" the authors show that this relatively new role is associated with commitment and expectations, while at the same time offering several advantages for both the individual users and their organization. The main benefit that the reference actors accrue is associated with a stronger relationship with the enterprise system vendor, which offers them (the users) the possibility to influence future product development strategies.

In terms of conclusions, the authors argue that there is a need to formalize this new role of reference actor so that the benefits of the referencing activities that are performed can be made explicit and valuable to the organization as well as to the individual user. At the same time, they identify five roles that the reference actor plays through: 1. Creating local comparability, 2. Help construct generic comparability, 3. Build a collaboration, 4. Establish proximity, 5. Foster the packaged enterprise system community.

as living documents. One interpretation of this is that the process does not really exist apart from the routine, and hence it would be futile to display it in a manner separated from the enterprise system. Another interpretation would be that there simply is not time to keep both the process maps and the routines up to date.

When the organization entered the maintenance phase with regard to their enterprise system, they made sure to assign one consulting resource one day every two weeks to visit the facilities and work on continuous improvements in the system and processes. The investment as such was not evaluated formally, yet the project was considered a success, despite its not achieving its objectives in the set time. In Figure 2.20 we summarize the case of Hestra.

In terms of the post-implementation phase of enterprise system implementations, there has been a substantial amount of research during the past decade. Earlier research did not assign any significance to this particular phase, yet more recent research has turned more to viewing the implementation as the first step towards a better ability to compete for the organization in question. In other words, after the implementation of a new

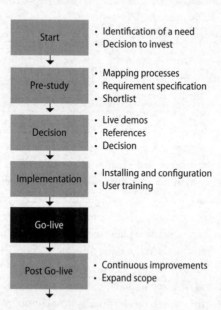

Figure 2.20 Summary of the Hestra case (adopted from Klingberg and Magnusson, 2011).

enterprise system, the organization is ready to start working on continuous improvements in an entirely different manner than before, having taken control of its processes and installing an information infrastructure that could suit not only the present but also future needs. This could be related back to the discussion from Carr (2003), about IT becoming an infrastructural resource rather than a strategic one.

With the investment being substantial, it has puzzled researchers that organizations have not been more prone towards evaluating the investment

Exhibit: Reasons for not conducting a post-implementation review

In a detailed study of why firms choose not to perform Post-implementation reviews of large-scale IT investments, Gwillim, Dovey and Wieder (2005) found some interesting results. With arguments such as "There is no impact", "The results would be obvious" there is not much we can do but consider the role of the post implementation review itself. Is it not a process of learning for future investments that we are embarking upon?

Other arguments such as "It would be hard to find the data" and "It would be hard to identify the benefits" relate more to issues of measurement, such as the argument of "It would be hard to find a base line". In regards to these issues, it may be a good idea to assess the progress in parallel with the implementation project itself not only in relation to the project goals of time, budget and scope, but also in terms of the overarching goals related to increased business performance. Would this not direct us towards identifying the performance-related goals at the start of the project and immediately starting to measure these in order to find a base line?

Perhaps the most worrying and troublesome arguments for not performing a post-process review are that "It would be embarrassing …" and "Then the benefits would be realized". With the investments being pushed as necessary and prioritized in the organization, the last argument signals an issue with IT Governance. In this situation it is possible to get your investment, such as a new CRM system for your sales and marketing, implement this with benefits to this part of operations and as the Sales and Marketing Director not having to pay for it. If we invest heavily without securing the realization of benefits through e.g. a reduction in head count and personnel costs, the benefits for the organization will not present themselves.

ex-post. Only 20 percent of IT investments are actually assessed ex-post, which could be considered eerily low given the size of the investments. In Exhibit we will devote attention to a study focusing on the reasons for the lack of ex-post reviews in more detail.

With the shift from large-scale to smaller-scale investments (in the wake of the disintegration of systems), coupled with the shift from CAPEX to OPEX and the alternative sourcing models for IT such as SaaS and Cloud Computing, the issue of ex-post assessments is, however, perhaps not as relevant today as it once was. If IT is something that you source as an operational expenditure, then any attempt at identifying the investment aspect of this would become futile. Subsequently, ex-post reviews would become obsolete, and merely a remnant of the past.

As seen in the Hestra case, the implementation was regarded as a step towards working with continuous improvements in the business. What constitutes the enterprise system is merely a means of getting things in order. Making the processes transparent and optimized (transiently), making sure that the organization from now on could implement new ways of working, adding functionality either through expanding the current system or through integrations to other systems in the form of web services et cetera. With the system being open to SOA based integrations, the functional scope of the system itself is no longer a delimiting factor. Instead, it could be regarded as a platform for securing continuous alignment between changes in business (primarily driven through external forces in the market) and the underlying IT support. This argument relates directly to that of McAffee and Brynjolfsson (2008), as previously reviewed. This does, however, introduce a blurring of the definition of platforms as presented in this book, but this is an issue that we will return to later on.

Exhibit: Advice as a driver of post-implementation job performance

In Sykes, Venkatesh and Johnson (2014), the study shows that there is a positive correlation between post-implementation advice and increased worker job performance. Focusing on the role of advice networks, i.e. networks of individuals geared towards offering advice to one another, the researchers found that in particular advice related to workflow and software had a positive impact on job performance.

In addition to this, the authors nuanced the role of advice into both "give" and "get", where they studied both the interplay between these two forms of advice and job performance, and their internal relationships. Here, the study highlighted the fact that there is an interaction between workflow and software get- and give-advice, as well as between software get- and give-advice.

The implications of these findings stress that organizations preparing for or currently working with their post-implementation need to understand the role that informal as well as formal advice networks play in increasing job performance. When choosing between software and workflow advice, software advice was perceived as key, resulting in a necessity of establishing and supporting this type of advice network from the start. For additional recommendations in terms of whom coworkers rely on for advice, see Lomi et al. (2014) and their study of boundary crossing in advice relations.

Recommended Reading

Cecez-Kecmanovic, D., Kautz, K., & Abrahall, R. (2014). Reframing Success and Failure of Information Systems: A Performative Perspective. *MIS Quarterly, 38*(2), 561–588.

Chang, J. Y., Jiang, J. J., Klein, G., & Wang, E. T. (2014). Do too many goals impede a program? A case study of enterprise system implementation with multiple interdependent projects. *Information & Management, 51*(4), 465–478.

Chang, S-I., Yen, D.C., Chang, I-C. & Jan, D. (2014). Internal control framework for a compliant ERP system. *Information & Management, 51*(3), 187–205.

Daniel, E. M., Ward, J. M., & Franken, A. (2014). A dynamic capabilities perspective of IS project portfolio management. *The Journal of Strategic Information Systems, 23*(2), 95–111.

Eisenmann, T., Parker, G., & Van Alstyne, M. (2011). Platform envelopment. *Strategic Management Journal, 32*(12), 1 270–1 285.

Eisenmann, T., Parker, G., & Van Alstyne, M. W. (2006). Strategies for two-sided markets. *Harvard Business Review, 84*(10), 92.

Etzion, H., & Pang, M. S. (2014). Complementary online services in competitive markets: maintaining profitability in the presence of network effects. *MIS Quarterly, 38*(1), 231–247.

Galy, E., & Sauceda, M. J. (2014). Post-implementation practices of ERP systems and their relationship to financial performance. *Information & Management, 51*(3), 310–319.

Gawer, A. (ed.) (2011). *Platforms, markets and innovation.* New York: Edward Elgar Publishing.

Grabski, S. V., Leech, S. A., & Schmidt, P. J. (2011). A review of ERP research: A future agenda for accounting information systems. *Journal of Information Systems, 25*(1), 37–78.

Polites, G. L., & Karahanna, E. (2013). The embeddedness of information systems habits in organizational and individual level routines: development and disruption. *MIS Quarterly, 37*(1), 221–246.

Rikhardsson, P., & Kræmmergaard, P. (2006). Identifying the impacts of enterprise system implementation and use: Examples from Denmark. *International Journal of Accounting Information Systems, 7*(1), 36–49.

Rubin, E., & Rubin, A. (2013). The impact of Business Intelligence systems on stock return volatility. *Information & Management, 50*(2), 67–75.

Subramaniam, N., & Nandhakumar, J. (2013). Exploring social network interactions in enterprise systems: the role of virtual co-presence. *Information Systems Journal, 23*(6), 475–499.

Sykes, T. A., Venkatesh, V., & Johnson, J. L. (2014). Enterprise system implementation and employee job performance: understanding the role of advice networks. *MIS Quarterly, 38*(1).

Tiwana, A., & Konsynski, B. (2010). Complementarities between organizational IT architecture and governance structure. *Information Systems Research, 21*(2), 288–304.

Tiwana, A., Konsynski, B., & Bush, A. A. (2010). Research commentary –Platform evolution: Coevolution of platform architecture, governance, and environmental dynamics. *Information Systems Research, 21*(4), 675–687.

Questions to discuss

- What are the main differences, from a user perspective, between implementing an onsite-, and a SaaS-based ERP?
- What are the main differences between an industry platform and a supply chain platform?
- Why do ERP related IT projects often fail to deliver on time, budget and scope?

PART II

In action

CHAPTER 3

Directing Enterprise System Platforms

Following our theater metaphor with the previous chapters on "Setting the Scene" and "Introducing the actors", this chapter covers issues related to directing the actual show. This could be criticized in line with Pinder and Bourgeois (1982), both on account of the metaphor misdirecting the attention of the reader, and the fact that we see very few examples of such an active agency as "directing" when it comes to the platform initiatives of enterprise system vendors. Despite this, we believe that directing holds in it an ample correspondence with the aspired activity, as well as more direct connotations than alternatives such as "orchestrating" and "leading".

Governance

This chapter covers issues related to how platform owners work with governing their Enterprise System Platforms. We start by presenting an overview of the different mechanisms that are prevalent, and then we discuss the implications of this particular model of platform governance for all the stakeholders involved.

THE PLATFORM GOVERNANCE MODEL

In the research project (Magnusson and Nilsson, 2013a, 2013b), we were asked to assess and aid in the development of the business model and governance of a Swedish ERP vendor's platform initiative. The ERP solution had existed since the 1990s and established itself well on the Swedish market with a 7 percent market share. The platform initiative focused on two parts. First, the deployment of a new environment for development, and second, the deployment of an app store for distribution and sales. With the platform initiative being driven by new technological capabilities, neither the business model nor the governance model was set. Hence this became the focus of our research.

Through a structured literature review, we identified a set of nine general governance mechanisms that were expected to be of value to this particular setting. Out of these nine, five were disbanded after the research project with regard to them not being representative of other platform initiatives. We will discuss these in turn in the following sections, with an introductory question and scale for each mechanism. These questions also function as a means for managers interested in initiating or assessing platform initiatives.

Price

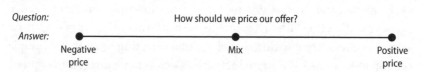

In the case of platforms, the traditional rationale of pricing has been highlighted as more complicated than within more traditional setups. The reason for this increased level of complexity lies in the multi-sided aspects, where network externalities and critical mass needs to be taken into account. In other words, the traditional perspectives of marginal cost of production, customer value et cetera is currently under revision.

In research there has been a substantial amount of work addressing the issue of pricing in platform settings (Amelio and Jullien, 2012; Chao and Derdenger, 2013). Eisenmann, Parker and Van Alstyne (2006) propose an alternative perspective to pricing in platform-mediated markets. Through looking at the two sides of the market as the "money side" and the "subsidy side", they show that the subsidy side is attracted by the money side, and the platform owner needs to set prices lower than they would on an independent market for the subsidy side. In terms of the money side, they need to set prices higher than they would on an independent market. The purpose of this is to create cross-side network effects where the money side will pay a premium for the width of derivatives. In the reversed direction, more money-side actors will create stronger incentives for joining the platform. Hence, we see pricing as an important mechanism for achieving critical mass. Following Esienmann, Parker and Van Alstyne (2006, p. 5), there are six factors that platform owners need to take into account (see Table 3.1).

Table 3.1 Overview of Factor, Issue and Example (Adopted from Esienmann, Parker and Van Alstyne, 2006, p. 5)

Factor	Issue	Example
Ability to capture cross-side network effects	Make sure to lock-in your users and avoid the possibility of them combining platform content.	Netscape's give-away of its browser to increase sales of their web servers. Without lock-in, users chose different webservers.
User sensitivity to price	Balance the different sides price sensitivity in order to increase demand	Adobe's licensing model with charging producers, not users of documents.
User sensitivity to quality	Subsidize the side of the market with a high sensitivity to quality; charge the side that supplies quality.	The high degree of royalty fees within the gaming industry. Through increasing the amount of users required for break even, this weeds out sub-par quality.
Output costs	In terms of give-aways, make sure that these unit costs are not substantial.	FreePC's attempt to give away PCs to users that agreed to view on-line advertising. Advertisers did not want to pay for advertising to customers that needed a free PC.
Same-side network effects	Avoid negative same-side network effects through exclusivity and segmentation of actors.	Covisint, the B2B marketplace for auto parts, failed to attract enough sellers since they did not want to be exposed to competition from other sellers in the same channel.
Users' brand value	Capture the loyalty of marquee users.	Visa's marketing strategy of attracting marquee users through subsidizing fees in exchange for them not joining competing platforms.

Pricing has long been emphasized as an important mechanism for solving coordination problems inherent in a platform business model. With the ambition to both create a critical mass of participation in the platform and to ensure coordination, platform owners have used what is often referred to as "negative prices", i.e. subsidizing one side (or aspect) of the market through premiums on another. According to Amelio and Jullien (2012), this is somewhat of a slippery slope, in particular when we take opportunistic behavior into the equation and consider that platforms may act in monopolistic or duopolistic markets.

One possibility of working with negative pricing is to work with bundling. Bundling in this manner refers to the joining of separate products/services into a single unit. In the case of a newspaper that without any increase in price bundles its product with a DVD movie, this could be considered as an instance of negative pricing. The impact of this has long been seen as detrimental to both the industries involved in the bundle, yet as Amelio and Jullien (2012) conclude, we need to take into account the issue of whether the platform on which the transaction takes place is in a monopolistic or duopolistic setting. In a monopolistic setting, this type of negative pricing will both increase the participation and the buyers' perception of quality, i.e. increase the utility and value of the platform. If, on the other hand, this is in a duopolistic setting, this will decrease the profits of the involved actors. The implication of this is that in a duopolistic setting, the opportunity cost of participating in the platform through taking part in bundling needs to be carefully considered.

There are two explanations of why firms get involved in bundling. First, there is the issue of price discrimination, where the firm can reduce valuation dispersion through one rather than several prices. Second, it is the issue of entry deterrence, where bundling acts as a means by which the firm makes entry into the market for competing firms more difficult (since it will necessitate the capability of delivering something that exceeds the scope of the competing firms. According to Chao and Derdenger (2013), bundling (once again in a monopolistic setting) will increase the value for all involved actors in the platform, and through price discrimination it will also lead to better market segmentation.

Revenue sharing

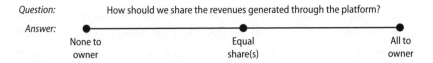

Question: How should we share the revenues generated through the platform?

Answer:

None to owner — Equal share(s) — All to owner

Under the assumption that the platform will be profitable, or at the very least drive revenue, the issue of revenue sharing becomes prevalent. One factor driving the complexity of this is the number of involved stakeholders in the platform. In the case of the iTunes App Store for iOS, the involved stakeholders that can be expected to share in the generated revenues consist of the innovators of the apps and the platform owners themselves. Here we see a distribution of 70 percent of the revenue going directly to the developing part, whereas Apple receives the remaining 30 percent as a compensation for services related to quality assurance of the apps and maintaining the app store/development environment. In 2013, a total amount of USD 10 billion of revenue was shared, resulting in a total net revenue for Apple of USD 3 billion.

In the case of enterprise system platforms, the complexity related to the involved stakeholders is higher. With the dominating business model for enterprise systems being sales and implementation through partner organizations, we have at least one more group of stakeholders that we need to take into account and make part of the revenue-sharing. In a case where the selling party is neither the platform owner nor the developing firm, there need to be sufficient incentive schemes and reward systems in place to drive sales. In the case of the platform initiative from the Swedish vendor in one of our studies, the revenue distribution was set to 50 percent to the platform owner, with the selling and developing parties sharing the other 50 percent on a more flexible basis. In the case of Salesforce and their platform initiative surrounding AppExchange, 85 percent goes to Salesforce if the developed app is solely for use among Salesforce customers, as compared to 75 percent if you target the larger market of non-Salesforce customers. This indicates that the vendor is subsidizing apps directed towards attracting new customers to the platform.

From these figures we see a clear difference between the revenue-sharing schemes of mobile devices such as the iTunes App store and Google Play and the enterprise systems such as Salesforce and NetSuite. One reason for this could be traced back to the difference in cost associated to quality assurance for the two alternative platforms. In the case of mobile devices, the vendors have been highly successful in creating a clear interface between the platform and the derivative products and services. The underlying infrastructure (the phone or the tablet) is relatively simple and non-critical for the business, at least when compared to an enterprise system. The enterprise system is highly complex and business critical, which makes any derivative solution wanting to integrate with it a potential risk that needs to be assured.

Another aspect of the difference in revenue generation between platforms for phones and tablets on the one hand and enterprise systems on the other is the difference between corporate and consumer settings. The enterprise systems are part of the corporate domain, and hence not subject to the same staggering level of innovation and agility. As discussed previously, the level of innovation within the consumer setting far outpaces that of the corporate, and hence there has so far been a lower demand for derivative products and services. We believe that this is but a temporary phenomenon, and with the increase of more and more enterprise system vendors turning towards the platform logic, we expect to see a radical increase in third-party activity.

Adding to the complexity even further, what about cases where users are actually part of the production of value? As we have noted previously, one of the main rationales behind the platform logic lies in the creation of network effects not only in a traditional supply chain manner, but also within each group of stakeholders. One of the main drivers behind the creation of a development environment for the Swedish ERP vendor that we studied lay in a necessity for increasing the level of innovation throughout the eco system. Before, the partner organizations (selling and implementing the ERP system) had a substantial amount of know-how and structural capital in the form of customizations and add-ons lying around. With this being part of what constituted their competitive advantage in relation to the other partners, they had previously been adamant towards sharing this with the rest of the ERP community. With the introduction of the new development environment, the ERP vendor promoted repackaging of this functionality into (more) easily integrated apps, with the underlying idea of increasing the sharing of functionality within the ecosystem.

As it turned out, the Innovators were satisfied with the new environment, yet the manner in which they used it never reached outside their own

Exhibit: The case of Gotheen Ltd

One of the firms that we have been involved in related to the enterprise system market is Shanghai-based Gotheen Ltd. This company was founded on the increased demand from western firms for establishing operations in Asia. With primarily Chinese localization as a service, Gotheen set up a Cloud Service Brokering between Western enterprise systems and local enterprise systems. For a firm establishing operations in China, there are a number of different aspects that need to be taken into account, such as local regulations, statutory reporting et cetera.

During one of our brainstorming sessions, a second avenue of revenue became apparent. With the enterprise system comprising functionality that was not utilized by the users (a recent study from Aberdeen Group showed that only 10–30 percent of the functionality in ERP systems are actually used), the firm could develop a CRM system through simply creating a new responsive interface to the functionality inherent in the underlying ERP. Compared to other competing CRM solutions, this would make it directly integrated with the rest of the firm's operations (and data) offering increased control and easy of implementation for the adopting firms. Hence, users that previously had been abhorred by the relatively complex interface of the ERP system for handling their CRM could be given a low-cost alternative, boosting the use of the ERP as well as shutting out competing CRM vendors.

So, how should the revenues be shared if for instance a partner organization sells the new CRM solution to a customer? How much of the revenue should go to the ERP vendor, Gotheen and the selling part? Or should the revenue go directly to Gotheen, with alternative value flowing to the vendor and the sellers in the form of sustained market share and revenue from add-on services related to implementation? As this case shows, revenue distribution is far from easy.

organization. The environment created an increased level of re-use within each firm, and a sharing of ideas that according to the partner firms increased their internal level of innovation. Having the possibility of sharing codes and apps between innovators created clear network effects, but these were limited to within each firm.

Turning this line of thought back to the users of the derivate solutions of the platform, we see issues related to rating, review and ranking as examples of how network effects are manifested. The users are more prone towards trusting other users than the sellers, and this begs the notion of a potential revenue-sharing between users as well. As in the case of Hotels. com, successfully connecting hotel guests with hotel providers is directly dependent upon the rating and reviews of the guests themselves. After fulfilling your stay at a hotel booked through Hotels.com, you are often asked to rate and review the hotel. In some cases, this results in you receiving a reward in the form of a discount on a future hotel stay.

Summarizing the mechanism of revenue-sharing, we find that it is contingent on the role and function of each stakeholder in the platform. In addition to this, it is related to issues we discussed during the section on Pricing, since revenue-sharing offers a complementing path to subsidization. In some of the platforms that we have reviewed, the substantial revenues exist on the outskirts of the platform, as consequences of activities enacted within the platform. As previously noted, enterprise systems licensing revenues constitute only a minority of the revenues when compared with consulting for customization, integration et cetera. Hence, this alternative or secondary stream of revenue needs to be taken into account as well. This is also related to the strategic imperatives of the involved stakeholders. For a vendor, market share and presence would be of more concern than direct revenue from the platform. As for the consultant in the form of an enterprise system vendor's partner organization, secondary sale of services would be the primary revenue channel. As for the third party innovator, it is unlikely that other sources of revenue would be available unless the packaging is done through SaaS or other subscription-based models, or through in-app purchases of added functionality.

Responsibility

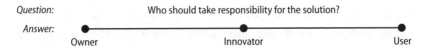

Question: Who should take responsibility for the solution?

Answer:

Owner   Innovator   User

Perhaps the most pressing issue in the cases of Enterprise System Platforms that we have studied is that of responsibility. How do we define the responsibilities of the involved parties? How can we define the interfaces between the involved parties to such an extent that it involves the issue of responsibility? Which level of responsibility offers the appropriate distribution of risk between the involved parties, without sub-optimizing the platform and obstructing the reaching and sustaining of critical mass?

As we found in our studies, this needs to be further addressed through a brief recollection of the involved stakeholders in the platform. Table 3.2 shows the rationales for each of the involved parties. With the delivery of the platform being an enterprise system, with critical functionality for the using organizations, the consequences of serious breakdowns in functionality are dire. Hence, the issue of responsibility becomes prevalent.

As noted in Table 3.2, all involved parties have strong rationales for avoiding responsibility over the derivatives. In the case presented in Magnusson and Nilsson (2013a), we reported on the rather ad-hoc manner in which this high risk was managed by the involved parties, i.e. the partner

Table 3.2 Overview of rationales and risks per stakeholder.

Actor	Rationale for avoiding responsibility	Risk
Owner	Limited control over the derivatives.	System failures may be traced back to faulty functionality in the enterprise system.
Innovator	Limited control and knowledge related to the existing installation and/or derivatives.	System failures may be traced back to faulty functionality in the derivatives or inadequate knowledge of the seller.
User	Limited control over both the existing installation and the derivatives.	System failures may impact business negatively.

firms of the enterprise system vendor. With the platform initiative being something that all parties saw as highly valuable and an interesting road ahead, they were adamant towards discarding the provision of derivatives to the platform. As third-party innovators, they assessed the future upsides as interesting enough to provide, at least in a restricted manner, the platform with a selection of derivatives.

However, the issue of responsibility was immediately identified as the most pressing of all business model related issues. Through the interviews, they expressed serious doubts concerning how they would be able to acknowledge any responsibility whatsoever, without having complete control over the installed environment. Hence, their main difficulty lay in the setup of having partner firms selling derivatives that they had not created themselves, to customers where they had incomplete knowledge of their installations. Notwithstanding this, the enterprise system vendor was clear in wanting to push responsibility away from their table, towards the developing party.

In this case, pricing was again used as a mechanism of governance where the third-party innovator priced the apps as close to zero as possible. With the enterprise system vendor having pushed responsibility to them, they agreed to take responsibility for the derivatives, but a responsibility matching a price of close to zero.

This brief case illustrates the difficulties involved in the setting of responsibilities within platforms where quality assurance is troublesome, and where the standardization of the underlying infrastructure (in the case of enterprise systems the individual system installations themselves) is incomplete. We will re-address this difficulty later on under the section on Control.

Control

Question: Which levels of control do we employ?

Answer: Bureaucratic   Intermediate   Ad-hoc

As previously noted, the capability of the platform for achieving critical mass is contingent upon the level of openness displayed in the platform. However, openness is very much a double-edged sword. We regard openness not as the opposing pole of control, but rather as one spectrum of the scale of control. Through this, issues of openness can be handled within the construct of control, something that we have found to be valuable.

Before we go into detail in terms of the control mechanism of platform governance, we need to address the aspects in terms of what control actually refers to in this setting. In its very distilled form, control refers to the activities designed to check that *actual actions* correspond with *planned actions*. This definition of control dates back to Henri Fayol and his early 20th century writings on administration, but as noted by Berry et al. (2009), the current definition(s) stray very little from the original.

In terms of controlling the Enterprise System Platform, we have noticed a sharp contrast between mature and less mature platforms in terms of which means of control they employ. As noted in our first study (Magnusson and Nilsson, 2013a), the prevalent means of control were associated with what Malmi and Brown (2008) would refer to as cultural controls, i.e. informal (see Figure 3.1). Even the contracts signed by the involved parties in terms of responsibilities and ownership were regarded as little more than ritualistic necessities, necessary for "upholding the front but in reality little more than a paper tiger", as noted by one of the respondents.

Controls directed towards planning were equally seen to be of little value, with the rationale that the initiative itself was a "shot in the dark", or a complementary strategy under testing. In terms of the Cybernetic controls, these were used but with little success. Budgets were made, measurements put

Cultural Controls					
Clans		Values		Symbols	
Planning		Cybernetic Controls			Reward and Compensation
Long range planning	Action planning	Budgets	Financial Measurement Systems	Non Financial Measurement Systems	Hybrid Measurement Systems
Administrative Controls					
Governance Structure		Organisation Structure		Policies and Procedures	

Figure 3.1 Management control systems package, adopted from Malmi and Brown (2008, p. 291).

in place et cetera, yet apart from the measurements in the app store itself there was no interorganizational sharing of information. The underlying reason for this was found to be related to the way that the initiative was perceived by the partners. Instead of seeing this as an external, market-facing initiative with substantial upsides, it was perceived as an initiative that primarily would help them to organize their development activities. The consequence of this was that the cybernetic controls had little effect on executing the strategy of the initiative as envisioned by the platform owner.

In a similar fashion, reward and compensation was not utilized as a means of control, or more precisely, did not become relevant. Since the innovators did not see the initiative as economically viable, they did not see potential financial upsides of the platform as feasible.

In a similar fashion, the administrative controls utilized in the platform were found to be under-utilized. With the business model not being set from the start, the governance and organizational structures for the initiative were not in place. Policies and procedures were set, but limited to quality assurance and the distribution of revenue.

Describing the case in the way seen here gives the impression of it lacking in maturity and structure. This is, however, not equal to saying that the control is sub-optimal for this particular setting. During the study, we were impressed with the openness with which the stakeholders discussed and collaboratively set the appropriate level of control. It was not perceived to be a process of blind consensus, but rather a careful dance in which the involved parties took great care in not upsetting the well-functioning collaboration taking place. This raises an issue where the origins of the platform initiative and the underlying rationale become critical prerequisites for designing management control.

For platform initiatives such as the extrovert Apple iOS or Salesforce. com, the means of control are radically different than in initiatives such as the more introvert case presented above. Looking at this from the proposed scale of bureaucratic versus ad-hoc controls, previous research in management control has shown that the level of bureaucracy is a function of size (Williamson, 1967). Organizations thus tend to become more and more bureaucratic in terms of control over time to counteract increasing coordination costs associated with increased size.

This would lead us to expect that newer platform initiatives will be more prone towards ad-hoc controls and as seen in the case, only to move later on more and more towards formalization. Unfortunately, this explanation only captures part of the issue. For the second part, we need to revisit the writings of Xue, Ray and Sambamurthy (2013) and their differentiation between exploitation and exploration. Platforms such as the one depicted in the case above would fall into the category of exploitation rather than exploration. The underlying rationale is not to approach a new market or to expand the existing market, but rather to reconfigure the existing market and make it more efficient. This also limits the upper size of the platform market, which makes issues related to bureaucratic controls (necessary for large organizations with potentially high coordination costs) less prevalent. In other words, they can "allow themselves" a lower level of bureaucratic control.

Based on this discussion, we can illustrate the relationship through Figure 3.2.

The aim of presenting Figure 3.2 is not to pinpoint the exact position of each of the platform initiatives, but rather to offer an example of how control could be placed into context.

Given this contextualization of control for Enterprise System Platforms, we turn our attention towards the *means* of control available to the different stakeholders in the platform.

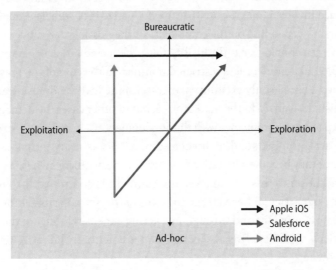

Figure 3.2 Overview of three platform initiatives in relation to strategic intent (X) and control (Y).

Table 3.3 Activities and means of control per stakeholder.

Actor	Activity	Means of control
Owner	Development, sales	Development environment, market environment, partnership
Innovator	Development, sales	Documentation, supply of derivatives, selection of derivatives
User	Selection, use	Selection of derivatives, factual use

The owner utilizes a series of means in order to perform control over the platform. The primary means is through the development environment, where automated controls make sure that the derivatives are good enough for the market and the risk of system failure is minimized. In a subsequent manner, the functionality available in the development environment also sets the scope for the derivatives themselves. This is controlled through the opening of new APIs that facilitate particular types of integrations. Hence, the owner both imposes restrictions in terms of notation and coding (through the choice of accepted coding languages/development platforms) as well as restrictions in terms of what is possible (given the available APIs).

In terms of the market environment, this is controlled through both the accreditation of partners that are allowed to publish derivatives, and the quality assurance involved in assessing that the derivative is of sufficient quality for the market. Depending on the complexity of the possible derivatives and the underlying technology (e.g. the ERP system), the accreditation of new partners is handled in a more or less restricted manner. In the case of the previously described example only existing partners with the ERP vendor were allowed to publish derivatives in the marketplace, but in other cases the demands are instead placed on compliance with the development environment's restrictions and separate contracts and/or direct fees for quality assurance. Hence quality assurance may become a lucrative business for the platform owner.

In addition to this, the market environment is controlled through the visibility of particular derivatives. In terms of the iOS app store, innovators can create campaigns and through marketing expenses influence their own derivatives' visibility. This also constitutes a potentially lucrative business for the owner.

The innovators also utilize certain means of control. One of these means is through their choice in the level of compliance with standards related for instance to documentation of their derivatives. In the previously described case, we saw several instances of innovators who expressed that complying with the standards of documentation would result in a loss of competitive advantages, and that they preferred to be the only seller of their own derivatives. Hence, they did not aspire for the network effects of other innovators selling or repackaging elements of their derivative, but instead actively avoided this through documenting less. The market environment in this case simply became a showcase for their existing customers.

The selection of derivatives becomes the last means of control for the innovators. With the stakeholder category of innovator also containing actors involved with selling (or perhaps rather helping to procure) derivatives developed by other firms to customers where they are currently working in the capacity of consultants, we can see examples where certain parts of the market remain invisible to the customers. They are instead encouraged to focus on a slice of the market that the consultant perceives as possible. The outset of this slicing of the market may be related to existing inter-innovator partnerships, the limitations of the consultants' own competence et cetera.

The user has two primary means of control: selection of derivatives and factual use. Where the selection of derivatives happens depends on the level of consumer orientation in the Enterprise System Platform. In most of the cases that we have reviewed, the complexity of the enterprise system itself and the consequent governance structures in terms of restrictions for added functionality or customization hinders a consumer-oriented market. In other words, the intended audience of the market environment is in most cases consultants and CIOs and/or a selection of technical personnel in the customer's organization. The end user is hence not the intended audience, which once again limits the rate of adoption and innovation within the organization. With Enterprise System Platforms achieving a higher level of maturity, we expect this to change towards the end user being the intended audience.

In terms of the factual use of derivatives, we see the end users as having the primary source of control. If the derivative does not add value to the end users' experience, it will be discarded. In previous studies the level of utilization of functionality from enterprise systems has been highlighted as being disconcertingly low, i.e. 10–30 percent. We expect the onslaught of new functionality through derivatives initially to lead to an additional decrease in this, provided that the user organization does not reframe the end user as the decision maker in terms of which derivatives should be added.

Business Models

A business has to be involving, it has to be fun, and it has to exercise your creative instincts.

RICHARD BRANSON

The interest in "Business models" came simultaneously as the hype around the Internet, starting in the mid 90s. The business model was at that time used as a way of communicating how firms would make massive profits by utilizing IT and the Internet, or as Michael Lewis (1999, p. 274) put it:

> Business Model is one of those terms of art that were central to the Internet boom: it glorified all manner of half baked plans. All it really meant was how you planned to make money. The "business model" for Microsoft was to sell software for 120 bucks a pop that cost 50c to manufacture. The "business model" for Healtheon was to add a few pennies to every bill or order or request that emanated from a doctor's office. The "business model" for Netscape was a work in progress; no one ever did figure out how to make money from Netscape; in its brief life Netscape had lost money. The "business model" of most Internet companies was to attract huge crowds of people to a web site, and then sell others the chance to advertise products to crowds. It was still not clear that the model made any sense.

Driven by the business community, the interest in the business model concept also took off in the academic community. A search of the term "business model" reveals a clear trend; Figure 3.3 illustrates the number of published articles in non-academic journals (PnAJ) and the number of articles published in academic journals (PAJ).

The burst of the IT bubble in 2001 did nothing more than ripple the interest in business models. Today, there is a widespread awareness in the business community of the need and importance of business models, but there is still significant confusion as to:

- What "it" really is?, and
- How, when and by whom "it" is to be used?

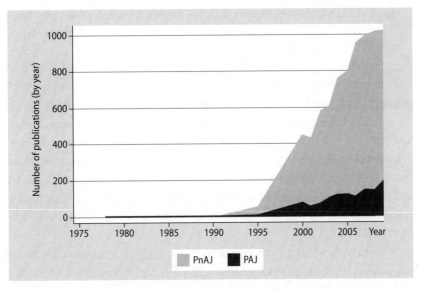

Figure 3.3 Source: Business Source Complete EBSCOhost Database. Period: January 1975–December 2009 (Zott et al. 2010).

In this chapter of the book, we will explain the origins of the business model concept, provide a set of useful definitions, give examples of business models and relate the concept to the context of Enterprise System Platforms.

> Whatever the mind of man can conceive and believe, it can achieve. Thoughts are things! And powerful things at that, when mixed with definiteness of purpose, and burning desire, can be translated into riches.
>
> HILL, 2011, P. 147

A business model is not a mathematical formula or some complex drawing; a (good) business model is in essence a (good) story (Magretta, 2002). The story explains how the company works; who the customer is, what the customer values, and how to make money. Magretta (Ibid.) provides an excellent example by telling the story of one of the most successful business models of all times, the traveler's check. The story starts during a European vacation taken by the president of American Express, J.C. Fargo, taking place in 1892. The story explains the trouble Mr. Fargo experienced in translating letters of credit to cash.

> As soon as I was on the road, my letters of credit were simply pieces of paper. If the president of American Express had this sort of trouble, imagine what ordinary travelers face.

The complete story includes precisely defined actors, believable motivation of actions, and a plot that turns insight into value (Magretta, 2002). In exchange for a small fee, the travelers could buy peace of mind (the checks were insured against loss and theft) and convenience (widely accepted by merchants). By accepting the checks, the merchants attracted more customers. More customers attracted more merchants. And the last beautiful part of the model is that the travelers always paid American Express for the checks in advance using cash, so there was no risk or credit cost for American Express; therein lies the economic twist.

The story shows that a good business model explains a better way of doing something than existing alternatives. The "better" may relate to the offer of increased value to a limited group, or the replacement of an old system with a new one. In the same sense, creating a business model is a lot like writing a new story. From one perspective, all stores are variations of old ones, a simple reorganizing of events unfolding universal themes of human interactions (Ibid). Following this train of thought all business models have two parts: part one focused on the making, designing or manufacturing of something, and part two focused on the selling of something. In this chapter, we will show how this statement does not hold true regarding platforms, and illustrate how it is possible to generate significant value building on another business model logic.

DEFINITION

> Everything should be made as simple as possible, but not simpler.
> ALBERT EINSTEIN

In order to provide an overview of previous business model definitions, we use the findings from Nenonen and Storbacka (2010).

Table 3.4 Definitions of business models.

Definitions	Reference
"A business model depicts the content, structure, and governance of transactions designed so as to create value through the exploitation of business opportunities"	Amit and Zott (2001)
"We offer an interpretation of the business model as a construct that mediates the value creation process"	Chesbrough and Rosenbloom (2002)
"Business model answers the questions such as who is the customer, what does the customer value, how do we make money in this business, what is the underlying economic logic that explains how we can deliver value to customers at an appropriate cost"	Magretta (2002)
"Business is fundamentally concerned with creating value and capturing returns from that value, and a model is simply a representation of reality. We define a business model as a representation of a firm's underlying core logic and strategic choices for creating and capturing value within a value network"	Shafer et al. (2005)
"We define the business model of a firm as a system manifested in the components and related material and cognitive aspects. Key components of the business model include the company's network of relationships, operations embodied in the company's business processes and resource base, and the finance and accounting concepts of the company"	Tikkanen et al. (2005)
"The particular business concept (or way of doing business) as reflected by the business's core value proposition(s) for customers; its configured value network to provide that value, consisting of its own strategic capabilities as well as other (e.g. outsourced/allianced) value networks; and its continued sustainability to re-invent itself and satisfy the multiple objectives of its various stakeholders"	Voelpel et al. (2005)
"The business model performs two important functions: value creation and value capture. First, it defines a series of activities, from procuring raw materials to satisfying the final consumer, which will yield a new product or service in such a way that there is net value created throughout the various activities. Second, a business model captures value from a portion of those activities for the firm developing and operating it"	Chesbrough (2007)

Tabellen fortsätter på nästa sida

Tabell 3.4 forts.

"A business model depicts the content, structure, and governance of transactions designed so as to create value through the exploitation of business opportunities. A business model elucidates how an organization is linked to external stakeholders, and how it engages in economic exchanges with them to create value for all exchange partners"	Zott and Amit (2007)
"A business model consists of four interlocking elements (customer value proposition, profit formula, key resources, and key processes) that taken together create and deliver value"	Johnson et al. (2008)
"The business model can then be defined as the structure, content, and governance of transactions between the focal firm and its exchange partners. It represents a conceptualization of the pattern of transactional links between the firm and its exchange partners"	Zott and Amit (2008)
"Business models are defined as configurations of interrelated capabilities, governing the content, process and management of the interaction and exchange in dyadic value cocreation"	Storbacka and Nenonen (2009)

We choose to follow Osterwalder's definition:

> A business model is a conceptual tool that contains a set of elements and their relationships and allows expressing the business logic of a specific firm. It is a description of the value a company offers to one or several segments of customers and of the architecture of the firm and its network of partners for creating, marketing, and delivering this value and relationship capital, to generate profitable and sustainable revenue streams.
>
> OSTERWALDER, PIGNEUR AND TUCCI, 2005, P. 2.

Osterwalder is a researcher who has made a valuable contribution to the understanding of business models by presenting his Business Model Canvas. By using his canvas, Osterwalder shows how different actors involved in the creation and definition phase of a business may interact in a structured way focusing on a set of specific aspects of the business. These aspects have been derived by Osterwalder as a common denominator from previous business model researchers and practitioners. In the next section, we will present a platform adaption of Osterwalder's canvas.

CONCEPTUALIZATION

All human knowledge concerning change starts with the ambition to model
the change object in question.

ZACHMAN, 1997

Every time we as human beings are involved in a task that is perceived as
non-trivial, we seek support in conceptual representations of the challenge at
hand. These conceptual representations can be drawings, schemas, models,
processes, frameworks, flow charts, to give some examples. Some of the
conceptual representations are formalized into standards with strict "rules"
regarding how to apply them; other conceptual representations are created
on napkins in restaurants accompanying interesting discussions.

The IT industry is packed with formalized conceptual representations
of various complex domains, as the IT workers' ability to *follow* formalized
conceptual representations and standards increase, the ability to build
bridges and work with previously separated entities also increases.

The IT industry is populated by many different competencies and
occupations, and in order to truly support value creation by IT, several different
occupations must collaborate. Collaboration between different occupations
means that it is not possible to use the "regular" conceptual representations in
use in a specific occupation; it is necessary to find more simple and pragmatic
conceptual common ground (Nilsson, 2013). Another way to put it is to say
that shared cognition precedes shared understanding (Ibid).

This also holds true with regard to business models. In order to create a
good business model, there are several key issues to be taken into account,
probably requiring several different experts. In order to put the experts to
good use, they must share a common understanding of the larger picture, and
be able to precisely communicate and position their respective contribution
in this larger picture.

Businesspeople don't just need to understand designers better; they need to
become designers.

ROGER MARTIN, DEAN, ROTMAN SCHOOL OF MANAGEMENT

4 Key activities	2 Value proposition	3 Relationships
• List Platform key activities (such as Connect platform partners via platform)	• Based on pains and gains, list value proposition from platform to respective partner (such as Newness, Design, Status, Price, Cost or risk reduction, Accessibility, Usability, Convenience)	• Describe partner relationship to the platform in terms of time, content and degree of complexity (such as transactional, long term, self service, SC)

1 Platform partners
• List platform partners (such as Platform owner, Platform content provider, Platform technical provider, etc)

6 Costs	7 Value Cocreation	5 Revenues
• List Platform cost types (such as fixed, variable, cost-driven, value-driven) • List partner cost types related to the platform (such as fixed, variable, cost-driven, value-driven)	• What is the secret ingredient? (scalability, critical mass)	• List Platform revenue types (such as brokerage, license, subscription, usage) • List Partner revenue types generated by the Platform (such as brokerage, license, subscription, usage)

Figure 3.4 Platform Business Model Canvas

THE PLATFORM BUSINESS MODEL CANVAS

The Platform Business Model Canvas (PBMC) is a slight modification of Osterwalder's very popular "regular" Business Model Canvas. The BPMC is comprised of seven key elements (see Figure 3.4):

1 Platform partners
   List all actors involved within or around the platform. This typically involves Platform Owner, Platform Innovators and Platform End users.
2 Value propositions
   What are the explicit value propositions? Each partner type must be connected to at least one value proposition.
3 Relationships
   Describe the kind of relationship that each partner type has to the Platform. It is common in Enterprise System Platforms for partners to have long-term, self-service relationships.
4 Key activities
   What are the key activities that are conducted on the platform?

5 Revenues

How will the platform generate revenue? What are the revenue types, and how to they relate to each respective partner?

6 Costs

What are the platform costs? What cost types are associated with each respective partner type?

7 Value cocreation

What is the twist/ secret ingredient? How is each partner type involved in the creation and delivery of value? How is value cocreated? Are there any possible network effects with adjacent platforms? How will the value cocreation from network effects be harnessed?

In order to understand how the PBMC may be used, we choose to show how the well-known Apple platform may be described using the model.

Key activities	Value proposition	Relationships
• Connect HW devices with innovative SW solution via platform • Market for SW • Development environment	• **Owner:** Fantastic community containing development and market environment • **Developer:** Innovative development environment for apps building to iPads/iPhones, channel to users via market • **User:** Innovative software apps at a very low price, easy to use, feedback, voting	• All relationships: self service, long term • **Owner:** Approves software, Maintaince platform • Content providers **developers:** Learning of dev. environment, Using dev. environment, complex, very time-consuming • Content providers **users:** easy/quick purchase, feedback, rating, sharing

Platform partners
- **Owner:** Apple
- **Content providers:** Independent software *developers*, professional and hobby
- **Content providers:** *users* of mobile devices

Costs	Value Cocreation	Revenues
• **Platform fixed costs:** Servers/maintenance • **Platform variable costs:** Approval of Apps • **Platform value-driven costs:** Business development • **Content provider fixed costs:** licenses, training	• The platform is connecting a large community of design-conscious people owning several Apple devices with the innovation power of a large community of software developers. Combination of offering access to a market channel with easy license model.	• Platform revenues: License, 30 % per sold App • Partner revenue 70 % per sold App

Figure 3.5 iOS BPMC from Ladhe, Magnusson and Nilsson (2013).

Through PBMC, it is relatively easy to conceptualize a complex platform strategy and use conceptualization as a foundation for communication. As platform initiatives to a large extent build on interorganizational arrangements, it is helpful to have a shared a conceptual model as structural support in the communications.

INNOVATION

The word "innovation" dates back to the 15th century and is broadly defined as the introduction of something new (Merriam-Webster).

However, this definition is not enough to encompass what is meant by "innovation" in today's society. In order to be called innovation or innovative, the "new" must also be perceived as useful. Within the business community, useful is closely related to value generation. We view the business model as the process of translating an idea or invention into a product or service that creates value or for which customers will pay.

As this view implies, innovation is a process, something that is done and/ or occurs and as a result produces something "new, useful and valuable". This activity can be done within a company, university or other formal institution, or it can be done in more informal settings outside organizations.

It is important to distinguish innovation from invention. An invention is usually associated with the attributes new and smart, but in order for an invention to become an innovation, there must also be a business opportunity and market.

All organizations must, at least to some extent, have the ability to innovate in the sense that they continually update and align their offerings with a changing and competitive environment. This need is highly present in the IT sector where there are short periods between innovative, IT driven solutions that redraw markets (Christensen et al, 2013).

From a policy perspective innovation is imperative as it is tightly connected to the creation of new jobs. The education system is occupied with how to educate and prepare tomorrow's workforce with competences that will stimulate and enhance the capacity for innovation. This is not an easy question as the ability to innovate involves a combination of skills encompassing human skills as well as organizational and business skills.

As presented in previous chapters, one of three key stakeholders presented in our platform model is the Innovator. We are referring to the person or organization conducting the process of innovation by complementing the platform via derivatives.

The process, or activity, of innovation has many faces, and may successfully follow many different patterns. Here follows a brief description of a few different types of innovation patterns aiming to provide the reader with a richer perspective.

Incremental innovation seeks to improve the systems that already exist, making them better, faster and cheaper.

Process innovation means the implementation of a new or significantly improved production or delivery method.

Red Oceans refer to the known market space, i.e. all the industries in existence today. In red oceans, industry boundaries are defined and accepted, and the competitive rules of the game are known. Companies try to outperform their rivals to grab a greater share of existing demand usually through marginal changes in offering level and price. As the market space gets crowded, prospects for profits and growth are reduced. Products become commodities, and cutthroat competition turns the ocean bloody (red).

Service Innovation can be defined as "a new or considerably changed service concept, client interaction channel, service delivery system or technological concept that individually, but most likely in combination, leads to one or more new service functions.

Business Model Innovation refers to the creation, or reinvention, of a business itself. Whereas innovation is more typically seen in the form of a new product or service offering, a business model innovation results in an entirely different type of company that competes not only in the value proposition of its offerings, but aligns its profit formula, resources and processes to enhance that value proposition, capture new market segments and alienate competitors.

Sustainable innovation or eco-innovation is a term used to describe products and processes that contribute to sustainable development

Frugal Innovation is about doing more with less. Entrepreneurs and innovators in emerging markets have to devise low-cost strategies to either tap or circumvent institutional complexities and resource limitations to innovate, develop and deliver products and services to low income users with little purchasing power.

Blue Oceans represent the unknown market space, i.e. all the industries not in existence today. Blue oceans are defined by untapped market space, demand creation, and the opportunity for highly profitable growth. In blue oceans, competition is irrelevant because the rules of the game are not set. Blue oceans can be created by expanding existing industry boundaries or by reconstructing industry boundaries.

Radical innovations (sometimes referred to as breakthrough, discontinuous or disruptive innovations) provide something new to the world that we live in by uprooting industry conventions and by significantly changing customer expectations in a positive way. Ultimately, they often end up replacing existing methods/technologies.

Disruptive innovation is an innovation that helps create a new market and value network, and eventually goes on to disrupt an existing market and value network (over a few years or decades), displacing an earlier technology.

Supply chain innovation is about applying best practices and technological innovations to your own supply chain in order to reduce such cycle and wait times and other waste (to use a Lean term) in your in-house processes.

The innovators surrounding a platform make up an ecosystem, or innovation system of stakeholders with the common denominator of building their innovations on top of a common core (the platform). This binds them together in terms that they collectively have significant power to influence the platform owner in a direction favorable to them. A "tight" ecosystem of innovators with similar interests as to the future development of the platform will experience significant network effects, or shared value creation by reinforcing each other's business, both in terms of influencing the platform owner, but also towards the end user, as their respective derivatives collectively attract a "tight" user community.

Within a well-functioning innovation system, there is an open and creative flow of ideas and resources that repeatedly come together in creative constellations producing new platform derivatives. It is an aggregation of human-, financial-, and creative capital building on a common platform vision. This may also be referred to as Open Innovation.

Exhibit: Who is Watson?

After building Deep Blue (a computer) that beat the best chess player in the world Garry Kasparov in 1997, IBM was in need of a new challenge that could bring their R&D team together. Deep Blue proved that it was possible to program a computer to "beat" a human given a narrow scope (a chess game), but is it possible to teach a computer to think, learn and become "smart"?

As a next step, IBM built Watson, a cognitive computer that can analyze and learn from large amounts of data. Watson was put to the test in the game of Jeopardy playing against the two grand champions. Watson understands and speaks English, and is not connected to the Internet.

Watson beat the two grand champions, and now IBM asked themselves: "Okay, so we have a decent computer, what the heck should we do with it?". The answer was to package and offer the Watson technology as a platform following a platform strategy.

Since 2013 is has been possible for innovators to utilize Watson's computing capacity to analyze huge data sets and answer very difficult questions. Watson's core technology is available via interfaces if the innovator complies with strict business procedures. Watson also has an investment group supporting the most promising innovators. In short, it is now possible for any entrepreneur to make use of a very advanced technology offered through a platform towards end users from a wide variety of industries.

Recommended Reading

Agrawal, A., De Meyer, A. & Van Wassenhove, L.N. (2014). Managing value in supply chains: Vase studies on the sourcing hub concept. *California Management Review*, 56(2), 23–54.

Constantinides, P. (2013). The communicative constitution of IT innovation. *Information and Organization*, 23(4), 215–232.

Majchrzak, A., & Malhotra, A. (2013). Towards an information system's perspective and research agenda on crowdsourcing for innovation. *The Journal of Strategic Information Systems*, 22(4), 257–268.

Parmar, R., Mackenzie, I., Cohn, D. and Gann, D. (2014). The new patterns of innovation. *Harvard Business Review, Jan–Feb*, 86–95.

Questions to discuss

- How can platforms be used to enforce governance?
- How would you design a platform governance model geared towards rapid reaching of critical mass?
- What signifies a viable governance model for an enterprise system platform?
- What constitutes an innovative business model?

CHAPTER 4

Platform Value Creation

With platforms constituting the bulk of value creation in the current economy, we will devote some time to exploring the exchanges of value as they occur in the platform. The basis for this exploration will be the previously presented conceptual model of platforms, and the analytical focus will be on the existing dyads of stakeholders. This choice in approach is in itself problematic, since it fails to address issues of cocreation of value as we have noted as being central to the very concept of platforms. The rationale for taking this binary or dyadic approach to value creation within platforms is purely pedagogical. With this book being intended as an introductory book on Enterprise System Platforms, the aim is to introduce the concepts to students of platforms.

There are a number of different methods for assessing the value through relationships, and in Nilsson and Magnusson (2013a; 2013b) we give an overview of some of the most prominent among these. The work in this chapter is inspired by the IEEE Value Encounter Model.

The Dyads of Value Creation

In Figure 4.1 we present the five dyads of value creation for platforms. The reason for not acknowledging the recursive dyad between the Owner and Owner is that in most of the platforms studied there was only one platform owner.

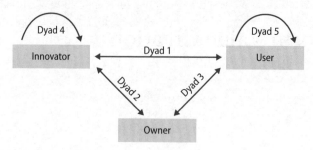

Figure 4.1 The Five Dyads of Platform Value Creation.

DYAD 1. INNOVATOR AND USER

The first dyad that we address is that of Innovator and User. In relation to Enterprise System Platforms, the Innovator constitutes a conglomerate of both pure-play third-party Innovators and consultants working with the appicifation of customizations. The User constitutes a conglomerate of end users and organizations.

From User to Innovator

In terms of the primary value received by the Innovator from the User, this takes the form of feedback and market presence.

Feedback refers to the rating and review conducted by the end users in correspondence to their use of the derivatives produced by the Innovators. This feedback fills several functions. First, it functions as a direct assessment from the intended market with regard to the actual value of the derivative. A low rating signals sub-par functionality and hence highlights the need for the Innovator to attend to this through either excluding the derivative from the market or improving it, based on information attained through the reviews. Depending on the market strategy of the Innovator, derivatives with low ratings may be excluded from the market or left lingering, depending on whether the Innovator assesses the negative attention from a sub-par derivative as being detrimental to their brand. The Innovator practices for this differ substantially between different types of platforms, depending on how much exposure the brand of the Innovator is allowed.

Second, feedback functions as a market mechanism for cross selling. With market places often having functionality for viewing more apps from the Innovator of a particular app, a high review is an avenue for boosting sales of other derivatives. Once again, this is contingent on the level of brand exposure of Innovator in the platform.

Third, the feedback also functions as a means for the Innovator to plan their development in new ways. Through the marketplace, they receive input for what the User wants and likes, and with a wide amount of derivatives in play, there is a steady flow of information in relation to how initiatives from other Innovators are received. From the Innovator perspective, this is both a curse and a blessing, since the high level of transparency coupled with the relatively low scope of each simplifies copying of concepts and ideas by other Innovators acting on the same marketplace. If an Innovator is highly successful, the time to market for competing derivatives will be short. Hence, we see tendencies for path dependence and "following the leader" emerges in successful platforms. From one perspective, this could be counterproductive for the User, since it narrows the innovative breadth of the derivatives in play. On the other hand, it allows for competition, where the traditional markup of "killer apps" becomes impossible. In other words, the high level of transparency functions as a means by which the price mechanism is straddled, leaving the User better off, while at the same time potentially decreasing the rate of innovation.

Market presence refers to the Innovator existing on a marketplace with their unique brand. Through the aggregated amount of users of their specific derivative(s) they acquire a presence, hence potentially opening up for additional sales through channels that are not platform-related. In the case of enterprise systems, the sales of a derivative for e.g. customs handling in the Far East may open up for a direct relationship between the User and the Innovator in question. Hence, the derivative becomes a window where the Innovator can signal their unique competence, where the derivative as such is only a part of the potential delivery. In the case of customs handling (an increasingly difficult issue, sic.), the Innovator may very well scope the derivative in such a way as it opens up for additional contracts for consulting and/or customized development.

In this respect, platforms offer a shortcut to market presence since the Innovators gain a direct channel through their derivatives to the complete set of users of the platform. The cost of customer attention is hence decreased

Exhibit: The construction of trust through rankings

In an article in Accounting, Organizations and Society, Jeacle and Carter (2011) approach the issue of how trust is constructed through features such as ratings, reviews and rankings. The empirical focus is the online travel website TripAdvisor. The authors argue that the independent travellers frequenting the site are subject to a calculative regime designed to elicit trust.

Following Giddens (1990, 1991), the authors state that social relations are disembedded, i.e. made possible to transgress both time and space. Ratings are considered instances of "symbolic tokens", designed to instill trust. Trust is considered both on the personal as well as the system level, i.e. between users and towards TripAdvisor.

As the results show, the simplicity and concreteness of the five-star rating system is in itself a mechanism for instilling trust in something objective, i.e. numbers rather than other types of information from travel agencies et cetera. At the same time, the rankings act as a means for legitimating hotels and other institutions, something that is becoming more and more apparent when they start to manifest their rating through physical signs in their receptions.

In concluding the calculative regime of rating, the authors discuss the implications of what they refer to as a "reverse panopticon", i.e. a situation where the many observe the few. The panopticon was first conceived by the British philosopher Jeremy Bantham (1748–1832) as the ultimate prison where the guard would be able to observe all the prisoners without the prisoners knowing whether they were observed or not.

compared to if the Innovator were to approach a free market without any existing relationships.

From Innovator to User

In terms of the value attained by the User from the Innovator, this is constituted of the Functionality of derivatives and Economies of Scope.

The primary value derived by User from Innovator consists of the functionality inherent in the derivatives purchased through the platform. These derivatives contain functionality of a smaller scope than the core as supplied by the platform owner, and through these they offer the possibility of a derivative-based customization and expansion of the core.

As previously noted, the very rationale of platforms lies in the possibility of easy access to functionality that expands the very foundation on which the said functionality is built. The derivatives offer the User the possibility, instead of as the previously so prevalent customizations of the core, of adaptation through selection. The User, exposed to the rich functionality through derivatives, can pick and choose that which best suits the required need. Hence, customization (with all the negative effects in terms of incompatible upgrades, loss of warranties, high risk of failure, substantial costs in terms of both time and other resources) is removed from the equation, or perhaps more accurately, transferred to a process of appification with the Innovator as the sole owner of risk.

This translates into the value of economies of scope. With customizations and new functionality transformed into derivatives traded in a marketplace, the User is now in a position where they can choose practically without risk and the loss of time. At the same time the structural soundness of the platform and the quality assurance taking place safeguards the derivatives working as intended, and perhaps more important in the case of Enterprise System Platforms, not risk operations. Hence, the User can access a wide variety of market-ready derivatives, which in turn leads to a diversified use of the core. In other words, the value that the derivatives from the Innovator add to the User is an increased possibility for diversification. In the case of handheld devices such as the iPhone, this opens up for a situation where the User can tailor their devices for highly personalized use. While one user may want to use the iPhone as a substitute for a ruler, a gaming console and a phone, another user will use it solely as a music- and video player.

In the case of enterprise systems, one user will use it for basic ERP support for their entire business process, while another will solely use it as a CRM system. With the investment in an Enterprise System Platform, the User thus opens up for not using the enterprise system as one specific thing, today and tomorrow, but as a platform on which functionality may be added and subtracted in correlation to the shifting needs of the business. This leaves the User in a position where previous difficulties of alignment between the possibilities of their packaged software and the changing needs of the business no longer exist. From this perspective, platforms come with the promise of (albeit through a capitalist market logic) facilitating continuous alignment and swift responsiveness.

DYAD 2: INNOVATOR AND OWNER

The second dyad is that between the Innovator and the platform Owner. As previously noted, we acknowledge that in most currently existing platform initiatives there is just one sole owner.

From Owner to Innovator

The value created by the Owner to the Innovator consists of revenue (cash), legitimacy, sense of community, economies of scale and visibility. We will address these in order, and also handle some of the adjacent questions such as pricing, revenue sharing et cetera as they become relevant.

In terms of revenue, the primary reason for the Innovator joining the platform in the capacity of third-party Innovators is that of potential revenues. These revenues are dependent upon both the pricing and revenue sharing taking place within the platform.

Turning our attention away from the monetary value exchanged from Owner to Innovator, the issue of legitimacy becomes important. Legitimacy is regarded as being in tune with external norms (Ashforth and Gibbs, 1990), and is hence related to how joining a platform initiative may impact the Innovator brand. Associating the brand of the Innovator with that of for instance Apple, Google or some other well-known brand will function as one way of adding to your legitimacy, piggy-backing the other brand if you so will. In other words, the Innovator has a choice in terms of which platform to join, and depending on their current strategy and customer base, this will be a choice related to the assessed value of the platform Owner legitimacy.

In smaller platforms such as that of Jeeves ERP or Netsuite ERP, this choice of which platforms to join coincides with what the Innovators see as their core business. If you are a firm with a long tradition of working with Jeeves, you will be more likely to join this platform than Netsuite. This is related to the wants and needs of your current customers as well as your current competence profiles. Within enterprise systems the required knowledge is still highly specialized, and turning towards a new platform initiative (with a new enterprise system as core) will be arduous and expensive. At the same time, a shift would result in customer attrition (or *churn*), and this is simply not a viable choice. With Enterprise System Platforms as well as the enterprise systems themselves becoming more and more easily accessible for third-party Innovators, this high threshold for "platform infidelity" will decrease, and we will see a situation where Innovators are more prone towards having a turnaround of platforms.

This development is, however, counteracted by another of the values that the Owner supplies the Innovator with, i.e. a sense of community. The communities for Innovators surrounding the different platforms that now exist differ in exclusivity and attraction. In some cases, such as that of the Enterprise System Platform that we studied in Magnusson and Nilsson (2013a), the sense of community was perceived as one of the core values from the perspective of the Innovators. They enjoyed being part of what they referred to as "the family" and despite being hefty competitors (between the Innovators) they considered other Innovators as colleagues and friends. With this being a local (national) ERP vendor, many of the senior staff had worked for the majority of other Innovators, and they knew each other intimately. When asked if they considered shifting to a different ERP vendor, all of the individuals that we interviewed responded that this would feel wrong.

In other words, the sense of community that exists among the Innovators is perceived to be a strong value that the Innovator attains through being part of the platform.

The third value that was identified from Owner to Innovator is that of economies of scale. With the platform being geared for economies of scale in development, maintenance and provisioning, the Innovator acquires a potential for economies of scale when joining the platform. In the case of the Enterprise System Platform we studied in Magnusson and Nilsson (2013a), the development environment was seen as the primary motivation behind moving towards the platform. Through a development environment where functionality and code could be shared among the development staff within each Innovator, this helped drive re-use of code and increase the efficiency of software development. At the same time, it allowed for transparency and overview of the current activities involved in coding, which was an added bonus for the management teams. In respect to the app store or external marketplace, these economies of scale were found in the low cost of publishing and entering the market with a new derivative. With sufficient control over the quality of derivatives, each new derivative holds a potential value in the marketplace, and hence adds value to the platform.

From Innovator to Owner

The value created by the Innovator for the Owner consists of a raison d'être, economies of scope and potential additives.

With the platform owner often (but not always) delimiting the core and opening up for open innovation within the ecosystem of the Innovator, the externalization of development of functionality that is essential for the User leaves the Owner in a difficult situation. In essence, the raison d'être of the platform is contingent upon the critical mass of the Innovator creating derivatives for the User. Without the Innovator, the platform would be without real value and subsequently fail.

In addition to this, the Innovator supplies the Owner with economies of scope, in a similar manner as they supplied the User with the very same. Economies of scope in this manner refers to the potential of the platform to cater to differentiated demands from User and hence attract the second element of critical mass, i.e. an adequate amount of users. At the same time, economies of scope for the Owner is also related to the possibility of identifying potential avenues for expanding the core, such as in the previously described case of Microsoft's inclusion of a media player in its operating system bundle. Through decentralized innovation with Innovator coupled with the ability to monitor the demand from User, the Owner is in a situation where they can identify additives for inclusion into the core. In the case of enterprise systems this could be in the form of functionality for e.g. social network analysis through the use of unstructured data from for instance Twitter feeds, or through integrations with the professional social network LinkedIn. This functionality can be swiftly identified and developed as an add-on derivative by the Innovator, and the statistics from use and downloads will give indications of when this should become part of the standard, core functionality. In other words, product development of the core is also externalized to some extent.

DYAD 3: OWNER AND USER

The third dyad is that of Owner and User. This relationship is characterized by a high degree of dependence in both directions, with the user being the primary driver of revenue for the owner, and the owner being the guarantor of functionality for the user. In cases where the platform is business critical, such as in the Enterprise System Platforms, this dependence is more apparent than in for instance mobile platforms.

From Owner to User

The value created by the owner for the user consists of functionality (of the platform), economies of scale and legitimacy.

In terms of the functionality, this refers to the value provided by the owner through the full scope of functionality available through the platform. This includes all derivatives as well as the marketplaces and technology of the platform itself. As previously noted, business critical platforms differ from those platforms directed more towards the consumer market (such as iOS et cetera) in terms of how the user perceives the lowest level of acceptable service. For an enterprise system, downtime is critical for business since it results in loss of business and substantial costs, while downtime on a game on the mobile platform may result in nothing more than nuisance and future avoidance of the said innovator.

The second value created by the owner for the user is related to the benefits associated with economies of scale in software provisioning. The platform offers the user a low-cost alternative to continuous provisioning, where new functionality can be efficiently added without difficulty. The ardent student will note that we refer to this as economies of scale and not scope, since the platform owner merely supplies the user with the necessary infrastructure for attaining economies of scale in their provisioning. As for the economies of scope, these are perceived as value attained through the Innovator-User dyad.

The last value received from the owner by the user is that of legitimacy. As previously noted, there are substantial positive effects of choosing a vendor with a high degree of legitimacy in the market. This has acted as a threshold for new, challenging vendors entering the market. In the case of platforms, this highlights a difficult situation where new platform owners are pushed towards strategies of cooption and envelopment since the thresholds for reaching a critical mass of users and innovators are substantial.

The choice of which platform to invest in is thus coupled with the continuous striving for legitimacy among the users. This highlights the role of platform branding, since one of the main values derived from the platform is related to increased legitimacy. It also highlights the difficulties with platform failures, where sub-par functionality in terms of the platform itself will have direct and massive negative implications for the owner.

From User to Owner

The value created by the user for the owner consists of revenue, markup of price, feedback and market share/presence.

The monetary value that the owner receives consists of revenue derived from both platform sales and the sales of derivatives. Hence, the user is also the primary customer of the platform owner. As previously noted, both pricing and revenue-sharing are important elements of platform governance. For consumer-oriented platforms such as Apple iOS, the revenues from the sales of derivatives constituted a staggering USD 3 billion in 2013, and in the case of the Enterprise System Platform Salesforce.com, as much as 85 percent of the revenues befalls the owner.

A second aspect of this monetary value derived from the platform can be found in the possibility of having a markup on the platform price itself. As in the case of Apple, they are able to infer a substantial markup on their iPhones due to the value derived by the customers from the access to apps and additional functionality. Comparing this to the pricing of other smartphones, we can see an additional stream of revenues coming from this markup.

In terms of feedback from the users, this constitutes the fourth value derived by the owner. Through engaging their customers in reviewing their products through the platform, they can control the quality of their services directly. Through their databases, they can amass enormous amounts of feedback from users, that will help them forecast the probability of a derivative or functionality in the platform being successful or not. At the same time, they can avoid bad press through the demarcation between derivatives and the platform itself. In the majority of platforms that we have surveyed, feedback is pushed towards the derivatives themselves, away from the core of the platform. Faulty functionality can be traced back to poor quality work from innovators rather than the owner.

The final value derived by the owner is that of market share and presence. Through the users, they acquire the necessary prerequisites for their continued existence. The existence of a large set of users (active or non-active) gives a means for the owner to communicate the merits and success of their platform. This can be seen in the marketing battle between iOS and Android, where figures of the total amount of downloads are used as an Archimedean point in the rhetoric. The vast majority of all downloads are not used and in addition to this are examples of freeware, i.e. apps without any associated cost and hence no associated revenue streams. This does not in any way discourage the owners from utilizing these figures in their marketing.

DYAD 4: FROM INNOVATOR TO INNOVATOR

The recursive relationship between the innovators constitutes the fourth dyad involved in the creation of value in platforms. This involves the information spillover effects of acting on the same transparent market, as well as the potential for joint ventures within both development and market activities.

In terms of the information-spillover effects, a situation where your offering as an innovator is immediately made available for your competition, along with the fact that fully transparent reviews in terms of sentiments from the market can be seen as threatening the very foundation of your business. Coupled with the potential flux of spinoffs of your derivatives that threaten to make your solution obsolete, this situation is characterized by entirely new codes of conduct and logic in respect of how you compete.

On the upside of all this lie the possibilities involved with a transparent market and short time to market. With the derivatives in many cases being highly delimited in scope, new strategies of cooption and envelopment surface, with ample new opportunities.

The innovators create value for other innovators through publishing their solutions on the open market, along with pseudo-open lists of their existing customers. At the same time, the number of users and the sentiments of these users are made available to the other innovators. In other words, the increased visibility of strategic intent among the innovators leads to a situation where the speed of competition is increased.

DYAD 5: FROM USER TO USER

The fifth and final dyad of value creation in platforms is the recursive relationship between the users. This relationship is characterized by the flow of information coupled with use between the users themselves. In the case of app stores, this information involves both reviews and ratings, as well as the underpinning information (number of downloads) used for various rankings by the platform owner. In other platform examples, this information is far less transparent and hence the network effects among the users are less apparent.

Figure 4.2 summarizes the five dyads of value creation according to the conceptual platform model.

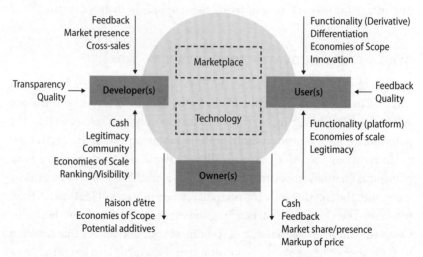

Figure 4.2 Value created in the platform.

Exhibit: Alfrek, The Research Market

During 2014, we became involved in a platform initiative where we utilize the findings from our research. The platform consists of a marketplace where researchers package their findings for distribution and sales to industry representatives. At present, we as a society spend an annual USD1000 trillion on research, and only a fraction of the results that this research generates is made available to the industry. Hence, the return on research has been highlighted as staggeringly inept, opening up for a new possible take on the interplay between industry and academia.

Alfrek (from the Norse god Mimer, the guardian of the source of all knowledge) is designed as a classical platform, catering to the needs of both researchers and industry representatives (i.e. two markets). Making it possible for the researcher to gain access to global distribution of her results (derivatives), with both feedback in terms of reviews and ratings as well as direct revenue, Alfrek opens up the previously closed box of science to the industry. The other side of the market, the industrial representatives gain access to leading ideas, directly packaged for easy consumption and integration. This increases the innovation capability of the customer firms.

Recommended Reading

Crane, A., Palazzo, G. & Spence, L.J. (2014). Contesting the value of "Creating shared value". *California Management Review, 56*(2), 130–153.

Grover, V., & Kohli, R. (2012). Cocreating IT Value: New Capabilities and Metrics for Multifirm Environments. *MIS Quarterly, 36*(1), 225–232.

Jacobides, M. G., Knudsen, T., & Augier, M. (2006). Benefiting from innovation: Value creation, value appropriation and the role of industry architectures. *Research Policy, 35*(8), 1 200–1 221.

Lavie, D. (2007). Alliance portfolios and firm performance: A study of value creation and appropriation in the US software industry. *Strategic Management Journal, 28*(12), 1 187–1 212.

Magnusson, J., & Nilsson, A. (2013a). Introducing app stores into a packaged software ecosystem: a negotiated order perspective. *International Journal of Business Information Systems, 14*(2), 223–237.

McNair, C. J., Polutnik, L., & Silvi, R. (2001). Cost management and value creation: the missing link. *European Accounting Review, 10*(1), 33–50.

McNair, C. J., Polutnik, L., Silvi, R., & Epstein, M. (2000). Outside-in cost and the creation of customer value. *Advances in Management Accounting, 9*, 1–42.

Salter, A., Criscuolo, P., & Ter Wal, A. L. (2014). Coping with Open Innovation: Responding to the Challenges of External Engagement in R&D. *California Management Review, 56*(2), 77–94.

Questions to discuss

- How would you motivate moving towards PaaS for an incumbent enterprise system vendor?
- What are the potential drawbacks for an innovator joining a platform?
- How does the distribution of value in a platform change over time?

CHAPTER 5

Conclusions and a call for research

As soon as some leading thinker comes up with an idea it is immediately pulled apart by the sympathies and antipathies generated: first its admirers rip large chunks out of it to suit themselves, wrenching their masters' minds out of shape the way a fox savages its kill, and then his opponents destroy the weak links so that soon there's nothing left but a stock of aphorisms from which friend and foe alike help themselves at will. The result is a general ambiguity. There's no Yes without a No dangling from it. Whatever you do, you can find twenty of the finest ideas in support and another twenty against it. It's much like love or hatred or hunger, where tastes have to differ so that each can find his own.

ROBERT MUSIL, *THE MAN WITHOUT QUALITIES*, 1995, P. 412

So, having spent the past decade studying the area covered in this book, we find ourselves hard pressed for supplying the reader with some conclusions. As researchers we have had the opportunity to communicate, in a piecemeal manner, fragmented conclusions through our academic publications, although we have so far swayed from aggregated conclusions. Such as in the opening quote by Robert Musil, this is an area where there is a tendency for dialectic movements where any attempt at stating a conclusion is immediately met by rebukes and counter-argumentation. We acknowledge the value of this method for pushing the envelope; yet we will allow ourselves the privilege of stating our conclusions in an absolute manner.

The past decade's development surrounding IT in general and enterprise systems in particular are captured in the introductory chapter of this book. With Digitalization, Commoditization, Standardization, Consumerization, Cocreation and Disintegration having been in full effect for quite some time, we can now see the general outlines of what type of a situation we are moving towards.

First, the picture painted in this book in terms of the user is one of great new expectations and opportunities. Never before have so many individuals had access to such advanced functionality. Never before has the cost of information retrieval and dissemination been so low. The effects of this can be seen in both the way that social interaction is being reshaped, as well as in the way that the delimitation between work and private life is changing. We are now in a situation where technology in many respects is democratized, and this in turn brings with it new challenges for organizations that wish to control their IT environments.

Second, the rise of platforms in general and Enterprise System Platforms in particular have a somewhat contradictory impact on the democratization of technology in the workplace. We see that the adoption of consumer-inspired solutions such as app stores for enterprise systems are dispersed in a manner following the incumbent rule and logic. The end users are not included in the list of individuals that can adopt new functionality. The end users are not catered to directly, but merely indirectly through proxies such as the office of the CIO and the IT department. This follows the same type of development as we described in Magnusson, Juell-Skielse, Enquist and Uppström (2012), where the adoption of SaaS business models by incumbent vendors was found to merely re-dress their previous business models into a new outfit named "SaaS". It was the ritual adoption as depicted in Meyer and Rowan (1977) all over again.

In other words, Enterprise System Platforms could be the missing link between an increasingly empowered group of users and the decline of corporate control of IT. Unfortunately, as we have seen so far, they are instead limited to being a new means of delivery for securing economies of scale and scope. This is not in itself a bad thing, yet we feel that the potential of the platform logic in enterprise systems is better than this. It brings the possibility of solving the tradeoff between user-driven and demand-driven innovation, where organizations striving for tapping into the creativity of their workforce would do well in pursuing a different path.

This brings us to our third conclusion, directed towards the role of the platform owner and enterprise system vendors themselves. Vendors that have now started to move towards PaaS and platform logic in the provisioning of their solutions will soon find themselves in a situation where they will want to retract. Most of the examples we have seen strive for platform dominance, and by this they misinterpret the possibility of becoming "the" platform in play. The existence of several, complementary platforms presupposes the complete interoperability of derivatives. Such as in the case of ERP systems, the strategy of "two-tier ERP", i.e. the acceptance of pluralism within one organization's stock of ERP systems, is still accompanied by severe drawbacks and difficulties. Interoperability is simply put not there yet, and the cost of integration is thus still an obstacle that needs to be surmounted. Without this being in place, Enterprise System Platforms will have to continue to compete in the same manner that they have historically competed. Hence, as a platform owner, you need to share the market with other platform owners, struggling in the same manner as you are in ascertaining dominance, whereby nothing has changed.

On an even more negative note, the move towards non-interoperable platforms will result in a situation where third party vendors will have to start making hard decisions in terms of which platform to pursue. With the gravitational pull of larger vendors, smaller vendors with local markets and fewer customers will draw the shortest straw. Opening up for PaaS may very well be a risk that they should not take, despite the many apparent benefits. Instead, they need to carefully consider strategies such as envelopment, where they de-bunk the excellence of their own, complete solution and start to see it as a derivative for the more established and dominant vendors. We soon expect to see vendors of smaller ERP solutions repackaging their solutions into add-on functionality for CRM systems.

Fourth and finally, for the innovator, the third party developer of derivatives, the move towards Enterprise System Platforms is more positive. We believe that despite running the risk of being pushed down in the value-chain by platform initiatives (be demoted to developmental partners rather than customer-facing partners), they will consider viewing the initiatives as interesting and positive. As noted previously, they will have to assess the long-term viability of their partnerships in a different manner than they are currently doing, but on the upside is the opening of several new markets. If they manage to reshape their expertise towards creating derivatives that are successful on one or several markets, they will also find ways of achieving substantial growth.

Enterprise systems will continue to be an important factor and element of any organization's IT environment. The disintegration of systems brings with it new constellations of partnerships, and new ways of consuming and provisioning the systems themselves, but at present we see no signs of the dominance of the larger vendors being threatened. Enterprise System Platforms are steadily emerging, with all the pros and cons of a new model, yet we believe it will continue to emerge and create new opportunities for owners, innovators and users alike.

Having said this, there is a strong need for additional research both in terms of platforms in general and Enterprise System Platforms in particular. The areas covered in the research that we have reviewed in writing this book leave many questions unanswered, and this constitutes a threat to the emerging market since it runs the risk of making unnecessary mistakes. Some of the areas where we see a need for future research include:

- Studies of the how incumbent vendors change their existing business models to cater to new technological prerequisites.
- Studies of the role of switching costs and technology debt in customer's preferences for pursuing new models of provisioning.
- Studies of how innovators choose which platform they wish to be associated with.
- Studies of platform viability over time.
- Studies of the role of industry analysts as instigators and drivers of changes in business model design.

POSTFACE

Enterprise systems can be seen as the ultimate sign of hubris within the information technology (IT) field: total systems, designed in a dictator-like manner to take precedence over business processes and render human-error and lead-times obsolete; adopted by organizations in a wholesale fashion during the past thirty-odd years, cementing economies of scale through *en-masse* computerization and digitalization. During the past decade, we have spent the bulk of our time studying this phenomenon. We have tried to avoid polemics about the benefits or drawbacks of the technology itself, and instead focused on its application in practice and theory.

The rationale behind writing this book is the current emergence of what could be referred to as a "turn to platforms" in enterprise systems. Platforms can, as described by Gawer (2011) be seen as a mechanism for combining economies of scale and scope. In respect to the emerging Enterprise System Platforms, these hold the theoretical potential of both agility and efficiency. If this promise holds merit, the implications are significant. If found wanting, the risk of "getting on the bandwagon" will be equally significant. This book is our attempt to sensitize the discussion on the merits and risks involved in Enterprise System Platforms and to open up for both an increased understanding and additional research into the field.

Stories of the platform strategy's supremacy over more traditional business models are many and hard to avoid. Apple's iOS and Google's Android ecosystems for smartphones and tablets sent shock waves through the market, making previously incumbent vendors like Nokia and their solutions obsolete. New vendors of enterprise systems, such as Salesforce within the Customer Relationship Management (CRM) market, apply platform strategies to externalize development and push the rate of innovation to unprecedented levels. These developments are repackaged as best practice by researchers, consultants and industrial analysts and marketed as "the new black". We acknowledge the perils of this potential fad.

When looking at the market for IT in general and enterprise systems in particular, we have found that it is easy to be swept away by the idea that change comes in a series of bursts (preceded by what Clayton Christensen would refer to as *disruptive innovations*) and sharp turns. Having studied the market in detail through the past ten years, we see this perception as being counterproductive in any real attempt at understanding what is happening. Instead, we choose to see the developments (both technological, social and business related) along the scientific principal of *Natura non facit saltum*. i.e. that all change is gradual in essence, not sudden. We believe that this principle offers guidance that helps us understand that changes occur in parallel, and that contemporary solutions are comprised of a long stack of previous as well as present solutions. Related to enterprise systems and their historical development, organizations today still host a multitude of "old" solutions as part of the installed base, used in combination with new solutions. Hence, the sharp turns existing in theory become much more ambiguous in practice.

In the light of this constant and ambiguous change, one might question the rationale behind attempting to capture these developments in the form of a book. In one respect, it can be compared to the arduous project set forth by Percival Bartlebooth in George Perec's epic "Life a user's manual". This character aspired for a project that should not be spectacular, based on coincidence or sustainability. Hence, for the first ten years he masters the art of watercolor painting. For the following 20 years, Bartlebooth travels the world and produces a painting of a new port every fortnight. These paintings are then sent to a master puzzle maker and turned into a jigsaw puzzle. For the last 20 years, he completes one puzzle every fortnight, only to have it transported back to the port in question and dipped into the ocean, erasing all traces of the painting and leaving only a white jigsaw puzzle. In writing this book we have had ample opportunity to revisit Bartlebooth's amazing project.

Throughout the book we have aspired to use a combination of hard facts stemming from research (both our own and that of our colleagues), and factoids stemming from stories and common perceptions in industry.

The reader will note that when the figures presented are hard facts, they are associated with a reference. The figures that are not associated with a reference are hence to be considered factoids, and should be regarded with caution by the reader. The reason for us incorporating factoids is that they are part of what could be referred to as "business savvy", and commonly used by industry. Hence, we feel that they have a dual purpose in both communicating general perceptions to the reader, and enriching the story through making it more accessible.

Throughout the book we use exhibits to highlight research and cases deemed specifically interesting to aid the reader both in understanding and to offer avenues for additional reading.

About the Underlying Research

In this book we have summarized the findings from our past ten years of research. This research has taken us into various fields and platform initiatives. Throughout these years, the majority of initiatives that we have studied have experienced drawbacks and setbacks. With this not being a criterion in our empirical selection, it highlights the difficulties associated with platforms. In the table below, we have summarized some of the most important (for our own understanding) projects that we have been involved in.

This research has allowed us to study a selection of interesting firms from a wide set of industries and to learn from how these firms are approaching the phenomenon of platforms. The organizations that we have worked with through our studies include IBM, SAP, Microsoft, KPMG, PWC, Accenture, Ericsson, SKF, Volvo, Stena, Evry, Agresso, Jeeves, Acando, Affecto, C Wonder, Qlikview and Hogia to name but a few. We owe the representatives of these (and many other) firms a debt of gratitude for allowing us to learn from their cases and experiences.

The research has previously been communicated to the academic community through the papers published in our names. A selection of these can be found in the reference list at the end of this book. In addition to this, we have continuously communicated our findings to the industrial community through keynotes at various congresses, trade fairs and seminars. We have also disseminated our findings and views through various trade press channels.

Project	Year (start)	Description
Plexus	2002	Project focused on creating a platform for interorganizational collaboration between SMEs.
Verksamt.se	2007	Project focused on establishing a single front office for public agencies involved in business startups.
Service Oriented Business Models for Enterprise systems	2008	Project focused on studying emerging business models such as Software as a Service and Cloud Service Brokerage among enterprise system vendors.
Munizapp	2010	Project focused on creating a mobile public e-service for case management.
Switching costs in public sector IT procurement	2011	Project focused on visualizing the switching cost effects of large-scale IT related investments within the public sector.
Smart City	2011	Project focused on establishing the prerequisites for a smart city marketplace.
JAM	2012	Project focused on supporting the creation of a business model for an ERP vendor's platform initiative.
Competing in Visualization	2013	Research program focusing on the use of interactive data visualization for increased efficiency and effectiveness.
e-Gov Lab	2014	Platform for e-government innovation and public private partnerships.
Alfrek	2014	Commercial project with the focus on establishing a marketplace for repackaged research results.

REFERENCES

Achebe, C. (1986). *Things Fall Apart.* Portsmouth, NH, and Oxford, England: Heinemann.

Agrawal, A., De Meyer, A. & Van Wassenhove, L.N. (2014). Managing value in supply chains: Vase studies on the sourcing hub concept, *California Management Review, 56*(2), 23–54.

Albert, S., & Whetten, D. A. (1985). Organizational identity. *Research in organizational behavior, 7,* 263–295.

Amelio, A., & Jullien, B. (2012). Tying and freebies in two-sided markets. *International Journal of Industrial Organization, 30*(5), 436–446.

Amit, R., & Zott, C. (2001). Value creation in e-business. *Strategic Management Journal, 22*(6–7), 493–520.

Anderson, C. (2004). The long tail. *Wired Magazine, 12*(10), 170–177.

Ashforth, B. E., & Gibbs, B. W. (1990). The double-edge of organizational legitimation. *Organization Science, 1*(2), 177–194.

Bala, H., & Venkatesh, V. (2013). Changes in Employees job characteristics during an enterprise system implementation: a latent growth modeling perspective. *MIS Quarterly, 37*(4), 1 113–1 140.

Banker, R., Hu, N., Luftman, J., & Pavlou, P. (2011). CIO Reporting Structure, Strategic Positioning, and Firm Performance: To Whom Should the CIO Report? *MIS Quarterly, 35*(2), 487–504.

Barrett, M., & Oborn, E. (2010). Boundary object use in cross-cultural software development teams. *Human Relations, 63*(8), 1 199–1 221.

Benders, J., & Van Veen, K. (2001). What's in a fashion? Interpretative viability and management fashions. *Organization, 8*(1), 33–53.

Benjamin, R.I., Rockart, J.F., & Scott Morton, M.S. (1984). Information technology: a strategic opportunity. *Sloan Management Review, 35*(3), 3–14.

Berry, A. J., Coad, A. F., Harris, E. P., Otley, D. T., & Stringer, C. (2009). Emerging themes in management control: A review of recent literature. *The British Accounting Review, 41*(1), 2–20.

Bharadwaj, A., Keil, M., & Mähring, M. (2009). Effects of information technology failures on the market value of firms. *The Journal of Strategic Information Systems, 18*(2), 66–79.

Borges, L. B. (1974). *Other inquisitions, 1937–1952*. Dallas: University of Texas Press.

Bresnahan, T. F., & Greenstein, S. (1999). Technological competition and the structure of the computer industry. *The Journal of Industrial Economics, 47*(1), 1–40.

Brown, R. H. (1978). Bureaucracy as Praxis: Toward a Political Phenomenology of Formal Organizations. *Administrative Science Quarterly, 23*(3), 365–382.

Brynjolfsson, E. (1993). The productivity paradox of information technology. *Communications of the ACM, 36*(12), 66–77.

Callon, M. (1998). The embeddedness of economic markets in economics. In Callon (ed.) *The laws of the markets*. Blackwell Publishers/The sociological review.

Carr, N. G. (2003). IT doesn't matter. *Harvard Business Review, 38*, 24–38.

Cecez-Kecmanovic, D., Kautz, K., & Abrahall, R. (2014). Reframing Success and Failure of Information Systems: A Performative Perspective. *MIS Quarterly, 38*(2), 561–588.

Chao, Y., & Derdenger, T. (2013). Mixed bundling in two-sided markets in the presence of installed base effects. *Management Science, 59*(8), 1 904–1 926.

Chang, J. Y., Jiang, J. J., Klein, G., & Wang, E. T. (2014). Do too many goals impede a program? A case study of enterprise system implementation with multiple interdependent projects. *Information & Management, 51*(4), 465–478.

Chang, S-I., Yen, D.C., Chang, I-C. & Jan, D. (2014). Internal control framework for a compliant ERP system. *Information & Management, 51*(3), 187–205.

Chesbrough, H. (2007). Business model innovation: it's not just about technology anymore. *Strategy & Leadership, 35*(6), 12–17.

Chesbrough, H., & Rosenbloom, R. S. (2002). The role of the business model in capturing value from innovation: evidence from Xerox Corporation's technology spin-off companies. *Industrial and Corporate Change, 11*(3), 529–555.

Christensen, C. M., Baumann, H., Ruggles, R., & Sadtler, T. M. (2006). Disruptive innovation for social change. *Harvard Business Review, 84*(12), 94.

Christensen, C. M., Wang, D., & van Bever, D. (2013). Consulting on the Cusp of Disruption. *Harvard Business Review, 91*(10), 106–114.

Cohen, M. D., March, J. G., & Olsen, J. P. (1972). A Garbage can model Organizational Choice. *Administrative Science Quarterly, 17*(1) 1–25.

Constantinides, P. (2013). The communicative constitution of IT innovation. *Information and Organization, 23*(4), 215–232.

Crane, A., Palazzo, G. & Spence, L.J. (2014). Contesting the value of "Creating shared value". *California Management Review, 56*(2), 130–153.

Cusumano, M. A., & Gawer, A. (2002). *Platform leadership*. Cambridge, MA: Harvard Business School Press.

Cusumano, M., & Selby, R. W. (1995). *Microsoft Secrets*. New York: The FreePress.

Czarniawska, B., & Sevón, G. (eds.) (2005). *Global ideas: how ideas, objects and practices travel in a global economy.* Malmö: Liber.

Daniel, E. M., Ward, J. M., & Franken, A. (2014). A dynamic capabilities perspective of IS project portfolio management. *The Journal of Strategic Information Systems, 23*(2), 95–111.

Davenport, T. H. (1998). Putting the enterprise into the enterprise system. *Harvard Business Review, 76*(4).

Davenport, T. H. (2005). The coming commoditization of processes. *Harvard Business Review, 83*(6), 100–108.

De Haes, S., & Van Grembergen, W. (2005, January). IT governance structures, processes and relational mechanisms: achieving IT/business alignment in a major Belgian financial group. In System Sciences, 2005. HICSS'05. Proceedings of the 38th Annual Hawaii International Conference on Information Science (p. 237b–237b). IEEE.

Dearden, J. (1963). Budgeting and Accounting for R & D Costs. *Financial Executive, 20.*

Dearden, J. (1964). Can management information be automated? *Harvard Business Review, 42*(2), 128–135.

Eisenmann, T. R. (2008). Managing proprietary and shared platforms. *California Management Review, 50*(4), 31–53.

Eisenmann, T., Parker, G., & Van Alstyne, M. (2011). Platform envelopment. *Strategic Management Journal, 32*(12), 1 270–1 285.

Eisenmann, T., Parker, G., & Van Alstyne, M. W. (2006). Strategies for two-sided markets. *Harvard Business Review, 84*(10), 92.

Etzion, H., & Pang, M. S. (2014). Complementary online services in competitive markets: maintaining profitability in the presence of network effects. *MIS Quarterly, 38*(1), 231–247.

Fischer, G., Giaccardi, E., Ye, Y., Sutcliffe, A. G., & Mehandjiev, N. (2004). Meta-design: a manifesto for end-user development. *Communications of the ACM, 47*(9), 33–37.

Galy, E., & Sauceda, M. J. (2014). Post-implementation practices of ERP systems and their relationship to financial performance. *Information & Management, 51*(3), 310–319.

Gawer, A. (ed.) (2011). *Platforms, markets and innovation.* New York: Edward Elgar Publishing.

Gawer, A., & Cusumano, M. A. (2008). How companies become platform leaders. *MIT Sloan Management Review, 49*(2), 28–36.

Ghazawhne, A., & Henfridsson, O. (2013). Balancing platform control and external contribution in third-party development: the boundary resources model. *Information Systems Journal, 23*(2), 173–192.

Giddens, A. (1990). Structuration theory and sociological analysis. In *Anthony Giddens: consensus and controversy, 1,* 297–315.

Giddens, A. (1991). Modernity and self-identity: self and identity in the late modern age. Cambridge: Polity.

Grabski, S. V., Leech, S. A., & Schmidt, P. J. (2011). A review of ERP research: A future agenda for accounting information systems. *Journal of Information Systems, 25*(1), 37–78.

Grover, V., & Kohli, R. (2012). Cocreating IT Value: New Capabilities and Metrics for Multifirm Environments. *MIS Quarterly, 36*(1), 225–232.

Grover, V., Jeong, S. R., Kettinger, W. J., & Lee, C. C. (1993). The chief information officer: A study of managerial roles. *Journal of Management Information Systems, 10*(2), 107–130.

Gwillim, D., Dovey, K., & Wieder, B. (2005). The politics of post-implementation reviews. *Information Systems Journal, 15*(4), 307–319.

Hakim, A., & Hakim, H. (2010). A practical model on controlling the ERP implementation risks. *Information Systems, 35*(2), 204–214.

Hald, K. S., & Mouritsen, J. (2013). Enterprise resource planning, operations and management: Enabling and constraining ERP and the role of the production and operations manager. *International Journal of Operations & Production Management, 33*(8), 1 075–1 104.

Hammer, M. (1990). Reengineering work: don't automate, obliterate. *Harvard Business Review, 68*(4), 104–112.

Hayes, D. C., Hunton, J. E., & Reck, J. L. (2001). Market reaction to ERP implementation announcements. *Journal of Information Systems, 15*(1), 3–18.

Hedberg, B., & Jönsson, S. (1978). Designing semi-confusing information systems for organizations in changing environments. *Accounting, Organizations and Society, 3*(1), 47–64.

Hill, N. (2011). *Think and Grow Rich: The Original Classic*. New York: John Wiley & Sons.

Jacobides, M.G. & McDuffie, J.P. (2013). How to drive value your way. *Harvard Business Review*, July–August, 92–100.

Jacobides, M. G., Knudsen, T., & Augier, M. (2006). Benefiting from innovation: Value creation, value appropriation and the role of industry architectures. *Research Policy, 35*(8), 1 200–1 221.

Jeacle, I., & Carter, C. (2011). In TripAdvisor we trust: Rankings, calculative regimes and abstract systems. *Accounting, Organizations and Society, 36*(4), 293–309.

Jensen, M. C., & Meckling, W. H. (1976). Theory of the firm: Managerial behavior, agency costs and ownership structure. *Journal of Financial Economics, 3*(4), 305–360.

Kallinikos, J. (2011). *Governing through technology: Information artifacts and social practice*. New York: Palgrave Macmillan.

Kensing, F., & Blomberg, J. (1998). Participatory design: Issues and concerns. *Computer Supported Cooperative Work (CSCW), 7*(3–4), 167–185.

Klingberg, J., & Magnusson, J. (2011). *User involvement during ERP implementation.* *Readings on Enterprise Resource Planning.* Montreal: ERPsim Lab, HEC Montreal.

Ladhe, T., Magnusson, J., & Nilsson, A. (2013). Introducing the Platform Business Model Canvas: Adapting an existing business model conceptualization to challenging institutional logic, 22nd Nordic Academy of Management Conference, Reykjavik 21–23 August.

Lavie, D. (2007). Alliance portfolios and firm performance: A study of value creation and appropriation in the US software industry. *Strategic Management Journal,* 28(12), 1 187–1 212.

Leavitt, H. J., & Whisler, T. L., (1958). Management in the 1980's. *Harvard Business Review, 36*(6), 41–48.

Leonardi, P. M. (2011). When flexible routines meet flexible technologies: Affordance, constraint, and the imbrication of human and material agencies. *MIS Quarterly,* 35(1), 147–167.

Lewis, M. (1999). *The new thing: a Silicon Valley story.* New York: WW Norton & Company.

Lomi, A., Lusher, D., Pattison, P. E., & Robins, G. (2014). The focused organization of advice relations: a study in boundary crossing. *Organization Science, 25*(2), 438–457.

Luhmann, N. (1995). *Social systems.* Palo Alto: Stanford University Press.

Magnusson, J. (2010). *Unpackaging IT Governance.* Göteborg: BAS.

Magnusson, J. (2013). Intentional Decentralization and Instinctive Centralization: A Revelatory Case Study of the Ideographic Organization of IT. *Information Resources Management Journal, 26*(4), 1–17.

Magnusson, J., & Bygstad, B. (2013). Why I Act Differently: Studying Patterns of Legitimation Among CIOs Through Motive Talk. *Information Technology and People, 26*(3).

Magnusson, J., & Bygstad, B. (2014). Technology Debt: Toward a new theory of technology heritage. Proceedings of the 22nd European Conference on Information Systems, Tel Aviv, Israel.

Magnusson, J., & Nilsson, A. (2013a). Introducing App Stores into a Packaged Software Ecosystem: A negotiated order perspective. *International Journal of Business Information Systems, 14*(2), 223–237.

Magnusson, J., & Nilsson, A. (2013b). Introducing app stores into a packaged software ecosystem: a negotiated order perspective. *International Journal of Business Information Systems, 14*(2), 223–237.

Magnusson, J., Ask, U., Oskarsson, B., & Gidlund, A. (2011). Measuring the impacts of ERP investments through post-implementation productivity development: An empirical analysis. 34th annual congress of the European Accounting Association, Rome, Italy.

Magnusson, J., Enquist, H., Oskarsson, B., & Gidlund, A. (2010). Get Together: A case of participatory ERP implementation and its transfer to class. International Conference on Computer Supported Education.

Magnusson, J., Juell-Skielse, G., Enquist, H., & Uppström, E. (2012). Incumbents and Challengers: Conflicting Institutional Logics in SaaS ERP Business Models. *Journal of Service Science and Management, 5*(1), 69–76.

Magnusson, J., Klingberg, J., Enquist, H., Oskarsson, B., & Gidlund, A. (2010). All Aboard: ERP implementation as participatory design. AMCIS Proceedings.

Magnusson, J., Nilsson, A., & Carlsson, F. (2004a). A conceptual framework for forecasting ERP implementation success: a first step towards the creation of an implementation support tool. International Conference on Enterprise Information Systems.

Magnusson, J., Nilsson, A., & Carlsson, F. (2004b). Forecasting ERP implementation success: Research in progress. European Conference on Information Systems.

Magnusson, J., Nilsson, A., & Hansen, L. (2012). Theatre of Creation: Industry Analysts as Propagators of Information Technology Frameworks. European Conference on Information Systems, ECIS, 2012 Proceedings, p. 20, Paper 48.

Magretta, J. (2002). *What management is.* London: Simon and Schuster.

Majchrzak, A., & Malhotra, A. (2013). Towards an information system's perspective and research agenda on crowdsourcing for innovation. *The Journal of Strategic Information Systems, 22*(4), 257–268.

Malmi, T., & Brown, D. A. (2008). Management control systems as a package – Opportunities, challenges and research directions. *Management Accounting Research, 19*(4), 287–300.

McAfee, A., & Brynjolfsson, E. (2008). Investing in the IT that makes a competitive difference. *Harvard Business Review, 86*(7/8), 98.

McNair, C. J., Polutnik, L., & Silvi, R. (2001). Cost management and value creation: the missing link. *European Accounting Review, 10*(1), 33–50.

McNair, C. J., Polutnik, L., Silvi, R., & Epstein, M. (2000). Outside-in cost and the creation of customer value. *Advances in Management Accounting, 9*, 1–42.

Meyer, J. W., & Rowan, B. (1977). Institutionalized organizations: Formal structure as myth and ceremony. *American Journal of Sociology, 83*(2), 340.

Meyer, M. H., & Lehnerd, A. H. (1997). *The power of product platforms.* New York: The Free Press.

Musil, R. (1995). *The Man without Qualities.* Translated by Sophie Wilkins and Burton Pike. London: Picador.

Nenonen, S., & Storbacka, K. (2010). Business model design: conceptualizing networked value cocreation. *International Journal of Quality and Service Sciences, 2*(1), 43–59.

Nilsson, A., & Magnusson, J. (2013a). The ERP App Store: Diverging and converging stakeholder interests in a PaaS ecosystem. Lecture notes in Business Information Processing, 16th International Conference, BIS 2013, Poznań, Poland, June 19–21, 2013, Proceedings. 157 (2013) pp. 38–49. ISBN/ISSN: 978-3-642-38365-6.

Nilsson, A., & Magnusson, J. (2013b). Value encounters in Platform as a Service: Informing the study of Value Cocreation. IADIS Information Systems Conference.

Osterwalder, A., Pigneur, Y., & Tucci, C. L. (2005). Clarifying business models: Origins, present, and future of the concept. *Communications of the Association for Information Systems, 16*(1), 1–15.

Parker, G. G., & Van Alstyne, M. W. (2005). Two-sided network effects: A theory of information product design. *Management Science, 51*(10), 1 494–1 504.

Parker, G., & Van Alstyne, M. (2010, June). Innovation, openness & platform control. Proceedings of the 11th ACM conference on Electronic Commerce (pp. 95–96).

Pawlowski, S. D., & Robey, D. (2004). Bridging user organizations: Knowledge brokering and the work of information technology professionals. *MIS Quarterly*, 645–672.

Pinder, C. C., & Bourgeois, V. W. (1982). Controlling Tropes in Administrative Science. *Administrative Science Quarterly, 27*(4), 225–245.

Polites, G. L., & Karahanna, E. (2013). The embeddedness of information systems habits in organizational and individual level routines: development and disruption. *MIS Quarterly, 37*(1), 221–246.

Pollock, N., & Hyysalo, S. (2014). The Business of Being a User: The Role of the Reference Actor in Shaping Packaged Enterprise System Acquisition and Development. *MIS Quarterly, 38*(2), 473–496.

Porter, M. E., & Millar, V. E. (1985). How information gives you competitive advantage. *Harvard Business Review*, (July–August), 1–15.

Pries-Heje, L., & Dittrich, Y. (2009). Looking at participatory design for means to facilitate knowledge integration. *Scandinavian Journal of Information Systems, 21*(2), 4–24.

Rikhardsson, P., & Kræmmergaard, P. (2006). Identifying the impacts of enterprise system implementation and use: Examples from Denmark. *International Journal of Accounting Information Systems, 7*(1), 36–49.

Robertson, D., & Ulrich, K. (1998). Planning for product platforms. *Sloan Management Review, 39*(4), 1–12.

Rochet, J. C., & Tirole, J. (2003). Platform competition in two-sided markets. *Journal of the European Economic Association, 1*(4), 990–1 029.

Rogers, E. M. (2010). *Diffusion of innovations*. London: Simon and Schuster.

Rom, A., & Rohde, C. (2007). Management accounting and integrated information systems: A literature review. *International Journal of Accounting Information Systems, 8*(1), 40–68.

Rubin, E., & Rubin, A. (2013). The impact of Business Intelligence systems on stock return volatility. *Information & Management, 50*(2), 67-75.

Salter, A., Criscuolo, P., & Ter Wal, A. L. (2014). Coping with Open Innovation: Responding to the Challenges of External Engagement in R&D. *California Management Review, 56*(2), 77–94.

Sarker, S., Sarker, S., Sahaym, A., & Bjørn-Andersen, N. (2012). Exploring Value Cocreation in Relationships between an ERP vendor and its Partners: A revelatory case study. *MIS Quarterly, 36*(1), 317–338.

Shafer, S. M., Smith, H. J., & Linder, J. C. (2005). The power of business models. *Business Horizons, 48*(3), 199–207.

Shapiro, C., & Varian, H. R. (1999). The Art of Standards Wars. *California Management Review, 41*(2), 445–460.

Simon, H. A. (1979). Rational decision making in business organizations. *The American Economic Review, 69*(4), 493–513.

Sledgianowski, D., Luftman, J. N., & Reilly, R. R. (2006). Development and validation of an instrument to measure maturity of IT business strategic alignment mechanisms. *Information Resources Management Journal* (IRMJ), *19*(3), 18–33.

Spinuzzi, C. (2005). The methodology of participatory design. *Technical Communication, 52*(2), 163–174.

Star, S. L., & Griesemer, J. R. (1989). Institutional Ecology, "Translations" and Boundary Objects: Amateurs and Professionals in Berkeley's Museum of Vertebrate Zoology, 1907–39. *Social Studies of Science, 19*(3), 387–420.

Storbacka, K., & Nenonen, S. (2009). Customer relationships and the heterogeneity of firm performance. *Journal of Business & Industrial Marketing, 24*(5/6), 360–372.

Strandgaard Pedersen, J., & Dobbin, F. (2006). In search of identity and legitimation bridging organizational culture and neoinstitutionalism. *American Behavioral Scientist, 49*(7), 897–907.

Subramaniam, N., & Nandhakumar, J. (2013). Exploring social network interactions in enterprise systems: the role of virtual co-presence. *Information Systems Journal, 23*(6), 475–499.

Suchman, M. C. (1995). Managing legitimacy: Strategic and institutional approaches. *Academy of Management Review, 20*(3), 571–610.

Sykes, T. A., Venkatesh, V., & Johnson, J. L. (2014). Enterprise System Implementation and Employee Job Performance: Understanding the role of advice networks. *MIS Quarterly, 37*(1), 36–49.

Taylor, J. C. (1998). Participative design: linking BPR and SAP with an STS approach. *Journal of Organizational Change Management, 11*(3), 233–245.

Tikkanen, H., Lamberg, J. A., Parvinen, P., & Kallunki, J. P. (2005). Managerial cognition, action and the business model of the firm. *Management Decision, 43*(6), 789–809.

Tiwana, A., & Konsynski, B. (2010). Complementarities between organizational IT architecture and governance structure. *Information Systems Research, 21*(2), 288–304.

Tiwana, A., Konsynski, B., & Bush, A. A. (2010). Research commentary – Platform evolution: Coevolution of platform architecture, governance, and environmental dynamics. *Information Systems Research, 21*(4), 675–687.

Upton, D. M., & Staats, B. R. (2008). Radically simple IT. *Harvard Business Review, 86*(3), 118.

Vilpola, I. (2008). Applying User-Centred Design in ERP Implementation Requirements Analysis. *Tampereen teknillinen yliopisto. Julkaisu-Tampere University of Technology.* Publication 739.

Voelpel, S., Leibold, M., Tekie, E., & Von Krogh, G. (2005). Escaping the red queen effect in competitive strategy: Sense-testing business models. *European Management Journal, 23*(1), 37–49.

Wagner, E. L., & Piccoli, G. (2007). Moving beyond user participation to achieve successful IS design. *Communications of the ACM, 50*(12), 51–55.

Wagner, E. L., Scott, S. V., & Galliers, R. D. (2006). The creation of 'best practice'software: Myth, reality and ethics. *Information and Organization, 16*(3), 251–275.

Weill, P., & Ross, J. W. (2004). *IT governance: How top performers manage IT decision rights for superior result.* Cambridge: Harvard Business Press.

Wheelwright, S. C., & Clark, K. B. (1992). Organizing and leading "heavyweight" development teams. *California Management Review, 34*(3), 9–28.

Williamson, O. E. (1967). *The economics of discretionary behavior: Managerial objectives in a theory of the firm.* Chicago, IL: Markham Publishing Company.

Woodard, C. J., Ramasubbu, N., Tschang, F. T., & Sambamurthy, V. (2013). Design capital and design moves: the logic of digital business strategy. *MIS Quarterly, 37*(2), 537–564.

Xue, L., Ray, G., & Sambamurthy, V. (2012). Efficiency or Innovation: How Do Industry Environments Moderate the Effects of Firms' IT Asset Portfolios. *MIS Quarterly, 36*(2), 509–528.

Yeats, W. B. (2010). *The Collected Works of WB Yeats, Volume I: The Poems.* Revised second edition. London: Simon and Schuster.

Yeow, A., & Kien Sia, S. (2008). Negotiating "best practices" in package software implementation. *Information and Organization, 18*(1), 1–28.

Zachman, J. A. (1997). Enterprise architecture: The issue of the century. *Database Programming and Design, 10*(3), 44–53.

Zittrain, J. L. (2006). The generative internet. *Harvard Law Review, 119,* 1974–2040.

Zott, C., & Amit, R. (2007). Business model design and the performance of entrepreneurial firms. *Organization Science, 18*(2), 181–199.

Zott, C., & Amit, R. (2008). The fit between product market strategy and business model: implications for firm performance. *Strategic Management Journal, 29*(1), 1–26.

Zott, C., Amit, R., & Massa, L. (2010). The business model: Theoretical roots, recent developments, and future research. WP-862, IESE. September. Available at: http://www. iese. edu/research/pdfs/DI-0862-E. pdf.

Zuboff, S. (1988). *In the age of the smart machine: The future of work and power.* Chicago: Basic Books.